TOP SCHOOL ESSAYS

Dr. B.R. KISHORE

GOODWILL PUBLISHING HOUSE®
B-3 RATTAN JYOTI, 18 RAJENDRA PLACE
NEW DELHI-110008 (INDIA)

Published by
GOODWILL PUBLISHING HOUSE®
B-3 Rattan Jyoti, 18 Rajendra Place
New Delhi-110008 (INDIA)
Tel. : 25750801, 25820556
Fax : 91-11-25764396
E-mail : goodwillpub@vsnl.net
website : www.goodwillpublishinghouse.com

Printed at : Kumar Offset Printers, Delhi-110092

CONTENTS

TOP SCHOOL ESSAYS

1. POPULATION PROBLEM

POPULATION explosion is one of our major problems. India is in the grip of population explosion, which has affected all our developmental activities very badly. The persistently high birth-rate and considerable decline in mortality rate have made India an overpopulated country. The problem is becoming more and more alarming with the passage of time. In terms of population, India is the second largest country after China. The infant mortality rate has come down to 80 from 126 per thousand. Life-expectancy, on the other hand, has considerably increased. This phenomenon has resulted in the rapid growth of the population of younger people. Similarly, there are an increasing number of men and women over sixty years of age Consequently, the clash of ideas and interests between the young and the old has become common.

There are about 18 million births every year in India. With this high fertility and decline in mortality, our population has already crossed the 1 billion mark. The enormity of the problem has been realised but commensurate steps towards population control have not been taken so far. The measures taken till date, to address this colossal problem, are really not adequate. Meaningful population control programmes should take into account such socio-economic factors as age of marriage, female literacy, rate of mortality, status of women and poverty because they have a strong bearing on our population explosion.

The growth of our population at the rate of 2% is really alarming. Every minute we have 45–50 additional mouths to feed. If this baby-boom continues, our country will soon be the most populated in the world and China will be relegated to the second position. This baby-boom reduces the quality and standard of living and increases the problems of unemployment, housing, health, family-welfare and education, etc. The problem becomes all the more worse because of illiteracy, ignorance, superstitions, religious and communal prejudices. Most of the people in villages and slums in the cities are totally ignorant of the evil consequences of a large and unplanned family. Owing to lack of proper awareness and age old traditions, coupled with superstitions, people in villages believe in divine dispensation in the moulding of their families and refuse to plan them. Small farmers and agricultural labourers, etc. have large and unplanned families because of the economic value of the children. The more the children, the more hands there are to earn for the family.

To achieve the desired aims and objectives in regard to population control and family planning, the status of women should be improved. They should be well educated and informed and economically independent, so that they can have control over their fertility. It is a fact that female literacy has a strong correlation with higher age of marriage and lower birth rate. Birth rate can be brought down by 12 per thousand if the mean age of marriage is raised to 20 years among women. It has been observed that seven years of schooling leads to a three-and-a-half-year delay in marriage and also lower infant mortality. Late marriages should be encouraged and child marriages should be dealt with strictly. Marriage registration should be made compulsory and no marriage should be considered legal without it. 'Two children' norm should be strictly implemented and there should not be any violation of it.

Unless population is controlled, neither can poverty be eliminated nor the living standard be improved. Under the Five Year Plans, more funds should be allocated for family planning, mother and child care and birth control programmes. More and more sterilisation facilities, coupled with increased monetary incentives, should be provided in villages and towns. Couples accepting family planning with one or two daughters should be provided proper insurance cover, ensuring their welfare in old age. Security and protection in old age should be ensured to such couples by the government and the society. A strong system of incentives and disincentives should be adopted to check this explosion in our population.

Poverty and ignorance are at once both the cause and effect of our rapid expansion of population. Along with rapid and proper economic development there should be proper awareness among the people about the desirability of family planning. A mass propaganda and education programme should be launched through the press, T.V., and radio, etc. to enlighten the masses regarding the many advantages of family planning, birth-control and late marriages. If the present baby-boom does not stop in the near future, it will be disastrous for the country. It is better that people use more and more means of sterilisation, loops, condoms, and oral contraceptives, etc. to check the menace of rapid growth in population before it is too late. We can learn much in this respect from countries such as China and Sri Lanka, etc.

More emphasis should be laid on employment, women's education, poverty alleviation and birth-control schemes. It is through these means alone that the concept of a small family can be popularised.

Poverty arising out of unemployment and under-employment is the major cause of large families. Family planning and economic development have a strong positive association. One cannot be achieved without the other. They are interlinked and inter-dependent. The experience of the developed countries in this connection is before us. In poor families, an additional child is considered economically desirable, because he or she can help in increasing the income of a family to some extent.

The moot question is why India has so far failed in its population control programme and family welfare schemes. The policy-makers, leaders, demographers, and health and family experts should come together and seriously ponder over the matter. We should review our population control programme so as to give it new direction and dimension with the active involvement of the various governmental, private and corporate agencies. Even small countries like Sri Lanka and Bangladesh have managed to reduce the total fertility rate faster than India. Every year there is an increase of 18 million in our population, which is equivalent to the total population of Australia. All the other states in India should try to emulate Kerala, where total fertility rate is just 1.8. Our total fertility rate at present is 2.9, which needs to be reduced by one percent point. Family planning and welfare programmes need to be turned into a people's movement. It is an established fact that this explosion in our population is the root cause of poverty, social tensions, urban squalor, crime, environment degradation and ever-increasing unemployment. ●

2. UNEMPLOYMENT PROBLEM

THE problem of unemployment is a harsh, worldwide reality. Even developed countries like the U.S., England, France, Germany, and Italy, etc. also suffer from this problem, but it is more pronounced in India. With the passage of time it has become worse. It has become a threat to India's economic well-being and social development. It is one of the major causes of our poverty, backwardness, crimes and frustration among the people. India is the second largest country after China in terms of population and manpower. But because of large scale unemployment, this manpower is not being utilised. There are capable and willing hands but there is no suitable employment for them and they are forced to remain idle.

The ever increasing number of job-seekers on the live registers of employment exchanges shows how alarming and serious this problem has become in recent years. But this only gives a rough idea of the problem because all the job-seekers and unemployed persons do not get themselves registered with the employment exchanges. Moreover, there are no employment exchanges in the villages and rural areas of the country.

There are millions of young men and women waiting for job opportunities. This chronic problem of unemployment is not confined to any particular class, segment or society. There is massive unemployment among educated, well-trained and skilled people, and it is also there among semi-skilled and unskilled labourers, small and marginal farmers and workers. Then there is under-employment. The jobs being created have miserably failed to keep pace with the ever increasing number of job-seekers. It is a problem which presents a great challenge to our leaders, thinkers, planners, economists, industrialists and educationists.

In the far flung areas, villages and towns, the problem is all the more acute, as there are thousands and thousands of workers and farm labourers who do not have their own piece of land to cultivate. Majority of our farmers too, have very small holdings. Consequently, they remain idle for many months of the year. This has resulted in a mass exodus from villages to the cities and large towns. It is because of this limitless unemployment that the majority of our population has been living below the poverty line. The problem of unemployment has also given rise to many other serious problems, like those of extremism and terrorism. We should not forget that an idle mind is the devil's workshop. Many a young man takes recourse to lawlessness, violence, anti-social activities, terrorism and extremism because of frustration arising out of prolonged unemployment and lack of proper job opportunities.

A frustrated and unemployed man or woman can prove a very dangerous person. He or she will never allow others to live in peace. Many of our law and order problems are directly linked with this problem of unemployment among our young men and women. They are full of energy, drive, and initiative. If not properly oriented, these are bound to explode into harmful and anti-social activities. Therefore, it is the need of the hour that the youth is suitably employed and its energies, capabilities and skills are harnessed for fruitful and nation-building activities. If this problem is solved, many other problems would be solved automatically. For a democratic country and a welfare state like ours, unemployment is a big curse, which can be eliminated to a great extent by proper manpower planning and creation of job opportunities on a large scale. If the rise of our manpower cannot be reduced, it becomes imperative that the demand for it is sufficiently increased by proper short and long term planning, both in public and private sectors.

There are many reasons that are too obvious to be ignored, as far as this problem is concerned. The rapidly increasing population, defective education system, slow growth of industries, neglect of cottage industries, and backwardness of our agriculture, etc. are some of the major causes of the problem. Defective long and short term manpower planning is another factor helping this problem to have a new dimension. There are a few other factors, which have contributed in worsening the situation, but they are not as major as the ones mentioned above.

Our education system should be reviewed and changed according to our present needs. Like factories, our universities, colleges and schools are still producing a rich crop of graduates who are fit only for white collar jobs in the offices. These graduates are fit only for such jobs as those of clerks, assistants, officers and bureaucrats sitting at tables in the offices. These matriculates, graduates and post-graduates keep adding to the growing list of the unemployed. These educated but unemployed youths, numbering millions, are a source of great anxiety and concern. Our education should be work-oriented. It should be such that it enables a person to stand on his own feet instead of depending on others. It is really an irony that our highly educated and trained personnel, like engineers, doctors, and scientists, etc., run after government jobs. They are not willing to start their own workshops, laboratories, factories and businesses. Our educated young men and women, instead of facing the challenges and creating suitable job opportunities through self-employment, are wasting themselves in the pursuit of routine and easy-to-perform government jobs. They depend too much on the government and lack the courage and inspiration to stand on their own feet. There should be greater emphasis on vocational education. There should be many more technical institutions and training centres. Indiscriminate and unplanned admissions in colleges and universities should also be checked. Higher education should be reserved only for those who really deserve it.

It is really shocking that our Five Year Plans have consistently increased the number of unemployed persons. It is because our planners have failed in taking a proper, long-term view of the problem. Due to defective planning and poor manpower management, there are jobs for which we do not have sufficient number of proper hands, and on the other hand, there are thousands and thousands of hands, for whom there are no suitable jobs. This has given rise to brain-drain and flight of our talented people to other countries in search of greener pastures. Our manpower planning should be based on objective analysis, facts and figures and other relevant factors. Our wrong priorities, planning and policies have resulted in dangerous gaps and holes in our various employment schemes. Due of lack of proper manpower planning, graduates and post-graduates of various disciplines are forced to settle for jobs quite removed from their education, training and aptitude.

The rapid growth in our population is another major cause of this problem. Every minute there is an addition of 40 or more people to our already unmanageable population. Consequently, the creation of job opportunities has not kept pace with the rapidly increasing population. Besides unemployment among educated young men and women, it is there among uneducated labour too. Every year there is an increase of over 4 million people in the labour sector. Rural unemployment is increasing rapidly, resulting in a great pressure on the land cultivation and cottage industries.

The ever declining trend in village industry and handicrafts has further worsened the situation. The indiscriminate expansion of education facilities at college and higher levels of education is a sheer waste of national resources. Our education should be totally restructured and made work oriented. We need more of technical education than liberal education. Education should teach a person to stand on his own feet, instead of depending on the government for a job.

Our industries too have lagged behind, thereby aggravating the situation. We have invested heavily in public sector industries, which have low employment potential, neglecting small and village industries. Indiscriminate automation and computerisation have also contributed to the worsening situation. Any expansion in industries should be closely linked with the immediate needs of the community. Without keeping this in mind no manpower planning can be effective and successful. The emphasis should be on proper planning and utilisation of our vast manpower. It is imperative that we seek people's solutions based on our ground realities instead of abstractions. There should be maximum utilisation of our industrial capacity but it should be based only on these principles.

Recently, there was much talk to make 'right to work' one of the fundamental rights, but nothing concrete has emerged so far. Moreover, it does not seem to be practical in a country like India with its vast population and dwindling natural resources.

To alleviate this problem of unemployment and under-employment in villages, a progressive employment scheme called Jawahar Rozgar Yojana was introduced in 1989. Over 440 lakh families living under the poverty line benefitted from it. More such schemes are needed to create gainful employment opportunities for scheduled tribes, scheduled castes and other backward classes and communities in the rural areas of the country. Only then will our efforts towards development and industralisation get the desired results. ●

3. FAMILY PLANNING

FAMILY Planning has been adopted as our national policy and a lot of money is being spent on it. Yet we are far from achieving our targets. India's population is increasing fast in comparison to its dwindling and depleting resources. This rapid growth of our population has resulted in a very high pressure on our resources of food, employment, housing, clothing, education and alleviation of poverty. With the phenomenal advancement in science, technology, medicine, health and physical-care, the mortality rate has come down considerably but the rate of birth has not come down commensurately. In the absence of effective control and check on our population, all our Five Year Plans and developmental schemes are bound to fail. As a result, about half of our population has been living below the poverty line. Millions of our fellow citizens are deprived of basic necessities of life while the gap between the rich and the poor has been increasing.

In spite of huge campaigns and well organised propaganda, the advantages of a small family have not been accepted by the masses. India consists mainly of villages and rural population. About 80% of its population lives in villages. They are mostly ignorant, uneducated and superstitious. They still regard children as gifts from God. They believe in luck and fate and believe that every newborn child brings its own luck. As such, they cannot be motivated to have planned parenthood with 'two children' norm. The much desired people's participation in the family planning and welfare programmes is not there. The majority of rural masses have yet to accept the various contraceptive methods of family planning and family welfare.

It is in keeping with our democratic set-up that the family welfare programme is a voluntary one. People are free to choose their own methods of family planning that suit them best. People are being involved in the movement through social institutions, voluntary agencies, social workers and people's representatives. It is good that no coercive measures are adopted but lack of people's involvement to a desired level has been a real source of concern to the people behind the movement. It is high time that some mildly drastic steps are also taken to curb our ever-increasing population. Unless and until we have proper check on our population growth, it is almost impossible to improve the quality of life and standard of living. The programme of family planning needs to be vigorously pursued.

During the Emergency some drastic and coercive measures were adopted, which were resisted by the people. They also resulted in the overthrow of the government, headed by Mrs. Indira Gandhi, in the general election. Therefore, it has been made totally voluntary. The programme includes maternal and child healthcare, their nutrition and family welfare. The various schemes related to family planning and welfare are implemented through the state governments, for which the Centre provides complete assistance. There is a network of primary health centres and sub-centres, in the villages of the country to popularise the movement. The number of these centres is being increased further. Nirodhs or condoms, oral pills, contraceptive jelly, creams, etc. are being distributed free of charge through these health centres and other agencies.

These are also available at subsidised rates at various retail outlets, chemist shops and pharmaceutical establishments.

Much improved sterilisation and tubectomy operation facilities now exist at various hospitals, dispensaries, and primary health-centres throughout the country. Special camps and campaigns are also being organised in villages and towns for this purpose. Financial and other incentives are also given to the people who voluntarily undergo these operations. Research activities are going on at Family Welfare Training and Research Centre, Mumbai, Central Health Education Bureau, New Delhi, All India Institute of Medical Sciences, Delhi in the areas of demography, reproductive biology and fertility control. In order to provide maternal and child health-care services to more and more women and babies, the post-natal programme has now been extended to over 1000 hospitals spread in villages and towns all over the country.

The raising of the minimum age of marriage to 18 for girls and 21 for boys, coupled with the legalisation of termination of undesired pregnancies have been steps in the right direction. The family planning and welfare programme in our country was launched officially in 1952 and since then, there has been commendable progress. There is a good deal of consciousness among the educated urban people about family planning and use of contraceptives and yet we can learn something more from China in this respect.

No doubt there is much and appreciable awareness among the people about family planning and mother and child healthcare. More and more people have come to realise the many positive advantages that are there in a small and well-planned family, and yet there is still a vast gap between awareness and acceptance of the various measures of family planning. To bridge this gap there should be a number of incentives and disincentives. A useful and progressive family planning programme should necessarily seek the help of more and more voluntary agencies, social workers, panchayat-members, village medical practitioners, caste elders, religious groups and village nurses and dais. What we need is an integrated and methodical approach to the problem. ●

4. EVILS OF DOWRY

DOWRY system is one of the major evils afflicting India. It is really a great curse and a blot on our nation and society. It is discriminatory against women in general and unmarried girls in particular. It reflects man's domination and superiority over the women, which is really shocking and condemnable. It is really sad that outdated and orthodox systems like dowry still prevail in Indian society. It reduces the bridegroom and his parents to the status of beggars and exploiters, and the bride's parents to that of helpless victims. It is high time that the evils of dowry are eliminated forever. Let us stop it before it becomes more and more menacing with the ever-increasing demands of greedy and evil-minded parents and relatives of a would-be bridegroom. There is no limit to greed and accumulation of wealth by such dirty means as demanding dowry from the parents and guardians of young, unmarried girls.

The evils of this major social sin are many and too apparent. Because of this evil, hundreds of deaths and incidents of bride-burnings are reported every year in our country. Many more cases of this nature do not come to light at all. When they fail to bring in sufficient dowry, in cash or kind, young brides are harassed, tortured, burned alive and humiliated by their unscrupulous in-laws. Such an evil is to be found nowhere else in the world. It is a matter of great concern and shame to all of us that marriages are being settled on the basis of the value of the goods and money offered by the parents of brides, in the form of jewellery, costly clothes, T.V., car, scooter, furniture, and refrigerator, etc. and hard cash.

This immoral and vile system has generated black money, corruption, greed and many financial malpractices, besides various psychological complexes. The unprincipled and unconscientious parents of a would-be groom try to justify dowry on the false presumptions that the newly married couple be given dowry to set up a new home and to begin a new venture. Such people do, however, condemn dowry in no uncertain terms when they have daughters to marry. This is nothing but a double standard. No doubt, dowry system is very old in India, and is perhaps as old as the institution of marriage itself but, certainly now it has lost all relevance, both social and religious. As such, the sooner it is eradicated the better.

In ancient days a girl did not inherit any property. Therefore, to compensate this loss, she was given several gifts in cash and kind by her parents, relatives, friends and well-wishers in dowry. These gifts ensured a sort of future security to the newly married girl. But now the situation has totally changed. Now women have equal rights. They have equal rights of succession and inherit property from their parents and ancestors. Now giving or receiving of dowry is a cognisable offence under the Dowry Prohibition Act. According to this Act, if any person who gives, takes or abets in the giving or taking of dowry shall be punishable with imprisonment which may extend to 6 months, or with fine which may extend to five thousand rupees, or both. Now, apart from the parents and relatives of the bride, the police and registered social organisations can also lodge a complaint against the party demanding dowry. Moreover, there is no time limit for lodging such complaints.

The laws enacted in recent years against the dowry system are very powerful and specific and yet they are not enough. They are being violated with impunity. There are thousands of cases of dowry every year but very few offenders are actually punished. In spite of these laws, the cases of dowry deaths are on the increase. Besides these legislative measures, we need other meaningful and effective social measures. All our efforts should be made to generate an effective public opinion against dowry system. More and more people, organisations, social institutions, leaders, religious heads and elders in the communities should be involved in the movement against this evil. The movement should be taken to villages and far flung areas of the country. The social and women's organisations should organise agitations against the parties indulging in demanding dowry. Social boycott and demonstrations against the offending parents and relatives of the boy can prove a powerful weapon in checking this evil. Moreover, the laws against dowry must be made more stringent so that the offenders may not get off scot-free.

To curb this evil, registration of marriage should be made compulsory, where both the parties are required to declare that they have neither taken nor given any dowry. Group and community marriages can also help in removing this evil to a great extent. Such marriage ceremonies can be solemnised in a community function in the presence of elders. In such marriages, there is no room for demand of a dowry.

Young women themselves should come forward and take the lead in this movement. They should never feel weak, helpless and feeble. They should recognise their strength, rights and potential. The weak is always exploited by the strong. They should refuse to marry when dowry is demanded. They should revolt and expose such anti-social elements. They should learn to stand on their own feet and try to improve their economic status in the society. It is heartening to know that there is a lot of awakening among the women folk of the country in the matter, but this is just the beginning. They should fight against all sorts of discrimination and unjust male domination. The young boys should also be made aware of the evils of dowry. They should reject their parents' plea of seeking dowry. What is needed is that the menace is fought both on the levels of law, and society. ●

5. MAN AND ENVIRONMENT

OUR environment is really unique because it sustains life and growth. On other planets there is no environment and, therefore, no life. Environment means all that surrounds us. It is a very complex and comprehensive phenomenon. It consists of the climate, geography, geology and all the natural resources that nature has bestowed upon us. Life is there because of our peculiar biosphere and ecosystem. There is life on this planet because of a certain balance between these various elements. Without this balance, our planet would have been just another sterile and lifeless planet revolving round the sun.

Our life depends on healthy and balanced environmental conditions. Our health, working habits, lifestyle, and behaviour, etc. are closely linked with all that surrounds us. The climate is an integral part of the environment. The varied climatic conditions on our planet have been responsible for all the variety that we have in our cultures, clothing, foods, festivals, and social customs, etc. The human population is scattered all over the world. But there are marked socio-cultural differences among the various races, groups, and countries because of different geographical and climatic conditions.

Existence on the earth presupposes maintenance of bio-diversity and the preservation of the delicate balance between the various elements that constitute our environment, geographical conditions and climate. Preservation and protection of environment means the protection of the earth, its atmosphere, and its various vital resources. These are the essential ingredients of our life and existence, and should be kept alive, pure, vibrant and rich. Of late, it has been keenly felt that their depletion can prove disastrous. For example, the depletion of the ozone layer of our atmosphere has caused a huge hole in the sky, which is growing bigger and bigger with the passage of time. Consequently, the very harmful ultraviolet rays from the sun are reaching the earth. This hole in the atmosphere was discovered over Antarctica. It has been caused by the release of chlorofluorocarbons (or CFCs) in huge quantity from chemicals mainly used in refrigerators and airconditioners.

There is a direct correlation between environmental conditions and our physiological functions. Change in climate affects our behavioural pattern in spite of our marvellous adaptability. For example, hot tropical climate and heat of the desert causes fatigue, exertion, lethargy and irritability. Similarly, very cold climates may cause inertia, morbidity and respiratory infections. Extreme climates and sudden change of environment have a direct influence on our lifestyle and work culture. Obviously, the conflict between environment and our so-called developmental activities is the main cause of so many of our problems. For example, for the conservation of our natural resources it is necessary that there is a proper check on our ever-growing population. The rapid growth in human population has adversely affected our land, forests, water, atmosphere, biodiversity and biomass. The overcrowding of our cities and towns, as a result of this explosion of population, is at the root of many of our evils. This has resulted in tremendous pressure on our agriculture, irrigation, forestry, energy and use of natural resources. Due to this imbalance, there has been a meteoric rise in crimes, diseases, squalor, poverty and misery. Our over-exploitation of the gifts of nature has created an unprecedented chaos in the environment. Our rivers are either dead or dying. The level of our groundwater is going down because of too much and indiscriminate pumping of water. Our earth has been green and wonderful, full of food and other goodies, and with other valuable boons of nature, but now it finds itself under an unbearable strain and stress because of our various acts of commission and omission.

It is imperative that we soon strike a balance between our environment and industrial development. Environment can no more be sacrificed for economical growth and development. Many of our power and industrial projects are still being implemented without proper environmental clearance. Our thermal power projects, based on coal, should be located far away from cities, towns, national parks, wildlife sanctuaries, lakes, coastal areas and places of historical, tourist and religious importance. And, a 5-km buffer zone is a must around such a plant. Moreover, there should be installation of all necessary pollution control mechanisms and devices for the treatment of waste products. Similarly, to check the environmental degradation in case of hydroelectric plants, there should be proper arrangements for treatment of catchment area and compensatory afforestation for the forest-cover submerged in the process of erection of such a plant.

To save the humanity from this looming ecological crisis, it is necessary that there is a mass movement against environmental degradation. The sooner we recognise this, the better. Our so-called industrial development, growth, and advancement at the cost of ecology is nothing but a regression, nay an 'ecocide'. Our oneness with nature and our environment is an established fact. Instead of fighting and destroying it, we should be with it because our fate as individuals is inseparable from the fate of Mother Nature. Our very survival depends on the survival and health of our eco-system. People should come forward voluntarily and participate in the movement to stop the over-exploitation of our rivers, oceans, lakes, forests, mountains, atmosphere and the earth. ●

6. ENVIRONMENTAL POLLUTION

TO pollute, literally, means to defile or make dirty. The addition of undesirable or unclean elements to the environment causes an imbalance and leads to pollution. This imbalance has not only led to deterioration in the quality of our lives but has also threatened the very survival of all life. If this imbalance grows beyond a certain limit, it may prove fatal. The ever and rapidly increasing pollution is a matter of global concern, because it is not confined to a particular country, region or land. It is a threat to the whole world and must be fought unitedly.

The problem of pollution is all the more acute in our overcrowded towns and cities. The ever-growing consumerism has further worsened the problem. The biosphere and ecosystem of cities and towns is fast losing its self-sustaining power. The rapid industrialisation of the cities has made them almost unfit for living. They are full of smoke, noxious fumes, dirt, dust, rubbish, corrosive gases, foul smell and deafening noise. The burning of various fuels in the factories and mills, release of a great amount of sulphur-dioxide in the air cause serious pollution. For example, in Delhi, a large part of the population suffers from respiratory and related disorders. In other metropolitan cities like Mumbai, Kolkata and Chennai, the situation is no better. The thousands of vehicles spewing smoke and producing unbearable noise in Delhi have aggravated the situation manifold. Delhi is symptomatic of the growing urban pollution and chaos in the country. The same fate awaits other cities of the country.

Since most of our cities are on the banks of the rivers or the coast, our rivers and seas too have turned murky and polluted and fishes and other creatures living in them are found rotting on the shores. The atmosphere in the cities is saturated with such pollutants as carbon monoxide, oxides of sulphur and nitrogen, hydrocarbons, pesticides, fly-ash, soot and sometimes, radioactive substances. The air is also choked with foul smells and toxic fumes. These have found their way into our foodstuffs. The toxic chemicals, industrial wastes and effluents discharged into rivers and seas from the mills and factories have proved fatal to marine life. Heaps of garbage, rising in ugly mounds in the cities, tell a story of our blind, foolish and lopsided urban growth and development. Our villages, too, are not free from this ecological degradation. They have lost much of their forests and pastures. This depletion of natural resources and imbalance in ecology will make our cities collapse under their own weight of contradictions.

Obviously, pollution has crossed all the tolerable limits and if no effective remedial measures are taken soon, the results may prove catastrophic. Vehicles belching smoke should not be allowed to run on the roads of the city. Eco-unfriendly vehicles should be strictly banned and there should be frequent pollution checks, and those found guilty of violating the rules should be adequately fined and punished. They must be forced to follow some absolute minimum standard of emission.

Noise is one of the great pollutants. The general noise level in the cities is rising alarmingly, causing many mental and physical diseases. Noise emanating from factories, vehicles, trains, public address systems, T.V. sets, aircrafts, and sirens, etc. is really too much. It has been proved that noise beyond a safe limit causes various kinds of disorders, both mental and nervous. Concentration is difficult in a noisy place, if not impossible. To perform anything creative and fruitful, concentration is a pre-condition. Noise also adversely affects our rest and sleep and thereby gives rise to many problems related to psychosocial behaviour. Frequent loud noise may cause decreased flow of blood in the small vessels, dilation of pupils, tension of muscles, digestive upsets, nervousness, anxiety and irritation. It lowers the working efficiency. The most glaring effect of noise is in the form of gradual loss of sense of hearing. There are noise-controllers but they are not of much help because of the lack of public awareness. We can reduce the menace to some extent by planting more and more trees.

The presence of pollutants in the sources of water, like rivers, lakes, ponds, and seas, is another great health hazard. Water reservoirs are full of pollutants, which include toxic chemicals, industrial effluents, suspended solids, organic and inorganic substances, and bacteria, etc. The sewerage has seriously damaged the health of our water resources. The discharges contain a variety of poisonous effluents, which cause the outbreak and spread of water-borne diseases and epidemics. The detergents, fertilisers, pesticides, oil spills are other major pollutants of water. Waste from slaughter houses, dairy and poultry farms, breweries, tanneries, paper and sugar mills have caused havoc.

In order to check water pollution, the sewerage and factory effluents and waste should be properly treated and cleaned before being discharged into streams, rivers and seas. Chemical industries should not be allowed to be located on the banks of the rivers and the coasts. There should be strict rules in regard to the observation of pollution rules and regulations, and the guilty should be severely punished. Gradually, people are becoming more and more aware of the growing problem of pollution. It is reflected in the first Act passed by the Indian Government in 1974, to have control over water pollution. Then in 1980 another Act was passed to prevent air pollution. And, finally, the Department of Environment was created as an independent agency in November 1980, to look after the environmental needs. But the measures, so far, to check environmental pollution have been more or less symbolic and half-hearted.

More than 70% of all the water available in our country is polluted. Like water and air, our soil is also getting polluted. It is estimated that over 35% of our total land area suffers from environmental degradation. Deforestation and excessive use of artificial fertilisers and pesticides are the main factors of this degradation of our land. Overgrazing has further worsened the problem. A number of solid wastes, such as garbage, trash, ash, sludge, plastic material, useless bottles, and cans, etc., dumped here and there make the atmosphere dirty and polluted.

In order to fight this menace, vigorous efforts should be made and anti-pollution laws should be strictly practised. More needs to be done through mass media in order to seek people's participation in the movement. Pollution holds out a great threat and danger to us and to the generations to come. Therefore, it should be fought tooth and nail. The use of solar and wind energy should be encouraged because it is clean and pollution-free. The awareness against the scourge seems to be growing but it needs to be matched with nationwide pollution control measures. ●

7. THE PROBLEM OF BRAIN DRAIN

BRAIN drain may be defined as emigration, especially from developing and underdeveloped countries to developed ones, by intellectuals, experts, highly qualified professionals like scientists, engineers, doctors, economists and other technically trained persons. It means depletion of intellectual, professional and technical resources of one country and enrichment of another. Almost all the developing and underdeveloped nations have been suffering from this problem since long. India is no exception. The problem is really very serious and must be addressed immediately. Thousands of Indian scientists, doctors, engineers and other highly qualified and trained persons have been immigrating to the advanced and developing countries of Europe and America. This exodus of our young, promising and bright professionals and scientists, to developed countries of the West, in search of greener pastures and better career opportunities, is a matter of great concern. The departure of these highly talented and trained people, forming the intellectural backbone of the nation, has a detrimental effect on the economic, technical, scientific and mental health of the country.

This huge outflow of our scientific, technical and managerial manpower is common and widespread in all the fields and professions, like medicine, engineering, education, technology, computer science, business management and human resource development. A big percentage of our national income is being spent on the education and training of these young men and women. And when they are in a position to serve the country, as highly skilled professionals and scientists, they migrate to rich and developed lands. This results in a great national waste in terms of money and manpower. It is nothing short of a national tragedy that these personnel, trained and educated at the expense of the Indian tax-payers, should leave the country at the very first opportunity. Moreover, the students who go abroad for higher education and research seldom come back. They leave their motherland and country of origin in the lurch and settle down in the West, enjoying a luxurious life. India has spent a great amount of her income and wealth in creating scientific, technological and educational infrastructure. But there are no commensurate returns because of this brain drain and outflow of talent. It also reflects our moral degradation and utter selfishness. It has a touch of treacherousness that many of our young men and women turn their backs on their beloved motherland because of the lure of money, comfort and better career opportunities. But they cannot be held solely responsible for this sorry state of affairs. No doubt, India has been spending millions of rupees every year on their training and education. But the matter does not end there. They must also be given opportunities for the best possible utilisation of their talents, skills, manpower and mental abilities.

The reasons for this massive exodus of our national talent are quite obvious. This one-way traffic is the result of a deep-rooted malaise, comprising of lack of proper employment opportunities, research facilities, job-satisfaction and recognition of merit and excellence. Many of our great scientists, like Hargovind Khorana, etc., emigrated to the West just because we failed to recognise their genius and did not provide them with proper research facilities.

The prevailing unemployment and under-employment are the other reasons for this brain drain. There are many young and talented scientists, doctors, engineers and technologists in our country who suffer from the lack of proper employment opportunities. Their patriotism is beyond any shadow of doubt but it will grow weak and wither away soon for want of nourishment and proper employment opportunities. No talent, however patriotic, can exist and prosper in frustration and unemployment. Many of our best boys and girls go abroad for higher studies and research. After the completion of their research and studies, they prefer to settle down there because they know that their capacities and capabilities would remain under-utilised here, and that they will not be provided jobs befitting their talents and training. If a few of them return, inspired by patriotism, national feeling and a high sense of duty towards India, they ultimately face frustration and unemployment resulting in great disillusionment and dissatisfaction. After enjoying the comforts, proper research facilities and affluence abroad, these young men and women are bound to suffer from frustration because of meagre salaries, inadequate research facilities, and poor working conditions in India. To attract our talented men and women back to India, it is essential that we create proper job opportunities, decent working conditions and top positions. It is almost impossible to stop this brain drain unless we considerably improve our living standards, salaries and other such facilities. In the United States, Canada, Britain or Germany, students can earn their living easily while learning. Besides, they are given sufficient support to continue their studies smoothly. But in India all these are lacking.

The problem of brain drain is really very serious and multidimensional. It cannot be solved with half-hearted measures and efforts. It has to be checked on two fronts. We should stop the outflow of our scientists, technicians, doctors, etc. by creating attractive, satisfying and meaningful job opportunities in the country. We should also create such conditions as may facilitate the return of those who have settled abroad. It is high time that we take concrete and immediate steps to check this brain drain because India is one of the worst hit countries by this intellectual exodus. India is bound to become a major world and industrial power sooner rather than later. The opening up of its economy and liberalisation of industrial and technological sectors will make it one of the most industrialised and scientifically advanced nations of the world. The multinational companies, foreign institutional investors and others are parking their huge funds in India. Consequently, the number of positions in industry, finance, science, technology, computer software, medicine, etc. are increasing considerably. And so, now each and every scientist, doctor, engineer, scientist, technologist and technician can take part in this noble task of taking the country forward. India is already a power to be reckoned with and soon there will be sufficient opportunities for our gifted and talented professionals and young men and women.

India should not only check the flight of talent but also lure back the thousands of our talented scientists, etc. from developed countries. In recent years the outflow of our talented personnel to oil-rich countries of the Middle-East has been a matter of concern. No doubt they earn and send back huge valuable foreign exchange, but the real loss to the country is in long term dividends and benefits as these people go there and settle for good. They seldom return to India.

It is in our best interest that this brain drain is checked and the outflow of talent is discouraged. It is really tragic that we fail to recognise our own talents and applaud them only when the developed and advanced countries of the West put their stamp of recognition and appreciation. It is high time that our leaders, government, educationists, planners, industrialists and others put their heads together to create suitable job and research opportunities so as to absorb our highly skilled, talented and gifted graduates and post-graduates coming out of universities, IITs, medical and engineering institutions. The need of the hour is that merit and excellence is given its due place of pride. Nepotism, bureaucratic interference, poor and appalling working conditions, etc. should be eliminated. Unless we create a proper work culture, working conditions, job opportunities and handsome salaries, it is almost impossible to check and stop this brain drain. The problem is really very serious and has also attracted the attention of the U.N. It has suggested that developing nations should be properly and adequately compensated for the loss caused by brain drain. The developed countries should pay the affected countries because it is a great boon to them. But the suggestion is neither practicable nor acceptable as it involves many complexities and controversies. ●

8. THE AIM OF EDUCATION

THE main aim of education is the all-round development of a student. Its purpose is to develop a student into a full, whole and integrated person. Thus, the objectives to be achieved through education and training are many and comprehensive. Education helps in achieving and developing skills, abilities, insights and scientific temper. Besides literary and aesthetic appeal of education, there are utilitarian aspects as well and they are equally important. Education aims at developing and bringing out the best of a student's inner personality, without neglecting the outer and material aspects. Education also means that students are made capable of standing on their own feet, to earn their bread and butter. An educated person is supposed to face the challenges of life bravely and successfully. No person can be called properly educated if he or she fails in making a meaningful contribution to the society and country.

The purpose of education is to strike a proper balance between inner and outer emotional and practical aspects of one's personality and life. If it is not done, it will result in an imbalanced development of a personality. It should help in flowering of both the spiritual and physical potentialities. All-round development means the growth and development of mind, spirit and body. All these are integral and interdependent aspects of a one's personality. It only means that there should be integrated development and none of these aspects should be neglected. Man is emotional as well as rational and both these aspectsshould be properly developed so as to form parts of an integrated and organic whole. The development of the one at the expense of the other will result in disaster. Man is neither a thinking machine nor a heap of emotions; he is not a bundle of flesh and bones. If one is guided simply by emotions, one's vision is bound to be distorted. Similarly, if one goes by reason alone then one would be a mere thinking robot.

The main task of education is to produce useful, intelligent, patriotic, emotionally integrated, morally strong, cultured, scientifically tempered and healthy young men and women. In short, the aim and objective of education should be proper integration and harmony between feeling, thinking and doing. Education should produce people properly adjusted with the rhythm of life, and this cannot be achieved unless there is the much desired adjustment between rhythms of mind and heart in the individual.

One of the primary aims of education is to develop character. Now, character is a very comprehensive term and means not only pattern of behaviour of an individual but also moral strength, mental presence, self-discipline, fortitude, and reputation, etc. Most of our modern problems have their origin in our lack of strong moral character. The modern age has been suffering from the crisis of character. If the character of the people is improved, many of the problems would take care of themselves. If the character of the people of a country is strong, it will be very easy to overcome any crisis, however great. It is said that if character is lost, everything is lost. What makes a man, really a man in the true sense of the term, is his character. Without character a man is nothing but a beast, a mere organism, just existing selfishly without any values and ethical sense. According to a poet, "Sow a habit and you reap a character. Sow a character, and you reap a destiny." Thus, the men of character are the men of destiny. Only those with strong moral characters have capabilities to control and guide the destinies of nations and the world. Mahatma Gandhi was such a man of character and so also a man of destiny. So were Gokhale, Tilak, Rajendra Babu, Vivekananda and Subhash Bose. The aim of education should be to make our students follow in the footsteps of these men of strong character and destiny.

The education imparted in our schools, colleges and universities should be such as to mould the personalities of the students, to enable them to face the realities of life with courage and confidence. In this context, the valuable concept of Basic Education championed by Mahatma Gandhi comes to mind. Basic education means that it should be based on work experience. It should not be theoretical and isolated but intimately related with a student's social and family background and relevant to the needs of the society. Work and training should form an integral part of education and not be an isolated activity. It should aim at producing artisans, craftsmen, doctors, engineers, technicians, teachers and other such professionals who may set up their own workshops, factories, mills, dispensaries, and schools, etc. and also fill up the vacant posts advertised by the government and other agencies. It only means that education should be work and employment-oriented. The essence of education and training lies in the removal of unemployment by producing skilled, talented and well-trained personnel and professionals. One of the main purposes of education should be to equip the people with means to face the problem of unemployment. No education worth its name can divert itself from the responsibility of providing suitable careers to people. This utilitarian aspect of education is as important as that of emotional and spiritual development. Education should also aim at achieving national integration and generation of stronger sense of unity and oneness among the people. In a country such as India, with such diversity, it becomes all the more vital. Every educated man and woman in India should be imbued with the sense of pride and honour for our common heritage, culture and history. It is this oneness of culture and heritage that has always stood us in good stead in times of crisis and catastrophe as a nation. Whether it was the Chinese aggression, Pakistani attacks or any other crisis, the whole nation rose like one to face it successfully. The cultural and emotional integration, effected through true and purposeful education, can very easily effect the singleness of purpose, leading to desired results.

The developed and advanced countries like Japan, Canada, France, Germany, and America, etc. are so, because they have been continuously investing heavily in education for the last many years. This clearly shows that education is an essential investment and input to realise the optimum output. The long term returns and benefits of investment in education, training and human resource development have been quite phenomenal, as is evident from the fantastic growth and development of these nations. Obviously, a purposeful education makes human resources and capital far more dividend-paying than it would be otherwise. Good moral character, scientific temper, self-dependence, patriotism, social and environmental awareness, single-ness of purpose, secular and broad outlook, fortitude and sense of human values, like compassion, truth, peace, non-violence, and charity, are some other aspects of education. ●

9. DROUGHT AND FLOOD IN INDIA

THE Indian sub-continent has a distinct geographical and historical identity. Its territories extend 3,214 kilometres between the extremes of the north and the south, and 2,933 kilometres between those of the east and the west. This vast landmass called India has been a playground of the monsoon from times immemorial. Monsoon is the seasonal wind of the Indian Ocean. By the end of the month of May, a low pressure is formed in the coastal plains in the west of India which attracts the monsoon winds and then there are occasional rains. In early June, the low pressure builds up heavily over north-western parts of the country and then the south-west rain bearing winds rush to the area with thunder, lightning and showers. By the beginning of July, these monsoon winds cover almost the entire country.

The intense heat of northern plains creates a low pressure area but the oceanic region maintains its low temperature and high pressure centre. Consequently, rain bearing winds, originating in the Indian Ocean, start blowing from the high pressure zone to the low pressure region over the vast landmass of India and then there are rains till September. The part of the monsoon winds from the Bay of Bengal move towards the plains of Ganga and Brahmaputra and cause heavy rains in West Bengal, Assam, Arunachal Pradesh and other neighbouring states of the sub-Himalayan region and the northern plains. But the distribution of rainfall is highly unequal. The Indian rains are erratic and ill-distributed, which causes frequent floods and droughts. The rainfall in India varies from place to place and year to year. The north-eastern states of Assam, Arunachal Pradesh, Meghalaya, and Nagaland, etc. receive very heavy rainfall. In contrast, Rajasthan and some parts of Gujarat have very low precipitation. The average yearly rainfall in these areas is between 100 and 500 mm. Between these extremes, there are low areas of moderately high and low rainfall ranging from 1,000 to 2,000 mm and 500 to 1,000 mm. Thus, some parts of the country are flood-prone while others are drought-prone.

Floods and droughts, both create havoc. The frequent droughts, particularly in Rajasthan, Gujarat and some other parts of the country due to lack of rain make the people and animals suffer a lot. For example, in the year 1987 there was widespread distress and suffering due to drought in many parts of the country. The worst affected were the small and marginal farmers, labourers and villagers without proper means of living and sustenance. Consequently, they lost jobs and incomes. There was acute shortage of drinking water as a result of the declining water table. People, in thousands, were forced to migrate to other parts of the country with their cattle and meagre belongings. Thousands of cattle-heads died for want of water and fodder as there were no crops at all.

To alleviate the suffering caused by frequent droughts, the Government of India and the states began a Drought Prone Area Programme (DPAD). Under this scheme these areas were divided into 615 blocks, spread over 91 districts of 13 states. This was done to achieve an integrated development of these zones through optimum use of land, water and livestock resources with a view to increase production, opportunities of employment and income of the people. The economies of these drought-prone areas was sought to be insulated from the effects of recurring droughts through diversification of agriculture, grassland development, soil management and conservation of resources of water. Similarly, there have been some very laudable attempts for integrated development of desert areas and arid zones of Rajasthan, Haryana and Gujarat. No doubt, the administration and the governments have been quite sensitive to the sufferings of the people of these areas and yet there is much left to be done and achieved. To remove the poverty of these regions and to alleviate suffering, more efforts should be made towards drip-irrigation system, dry land farming, conservation of forests and grasslands, stabilisation of sand-dunes, wise use of water resources, exploitation of non-conventional sources of energy and development of agriculture, horticulture and animal husbandry.

The uncertainty of the monsoon and the rains is well known. On the one hand, the lack of rains causes drought while on the other, its excess results in deluge and floods. Both the extreme states are undesirable as they cause a lot of suffering and loss of lives and material. In India, floods are an annual occurrence, occuring in one part of the country or another. Come rains and the rivers are in flood, causing havoc. The torrential and continuous rains give rise to floods which, in turn, inundate fields, forests, villages and towns, wash away river banks, trees, crops and cattle in their fury. They often change the course of the rivers and, thus, submerge much valuable agricultural, pasture and residential land. During the monsoon, the very life-giving rivers, like Brahmaputra, the Ganga and the Jamuna in the plains of Uttar Pradesh and Bihar, the Godavari, the Krishna, the Mahanadi, the Narmada and the Cauvery in the south, receive very heavy rainfall and discharge the maximum quantity of water resulting in frequent heavy floods. The southern rivers are comparatively less prone to floods, but they too are often in spate and cause extensive damage. The Himalayan rivers like the Ganga, the Jamuna, and the Brahmaputra, etc. are snow-fed and perennial and may rise in spate when there is heavy melting of snow in the higher regions in the summers. No doubt, most of the causes of floods can be attributed to nature. Very heavy rainfall in the catchment area, siltation of river-beds, land-slides in the mountains and hills, etc. are some of the main reasons of floods. But man's contribution to the recurrence of floods is no less. The indiscriminate cutting of trees for timber, destruction of forests and grasslands and greedy exploitation of the hills and mountains for minerals, etc. are also major factors of recurring floods. Construction of big dams, submerging vast tracts of forest land and woods also adds to the recurrence of floods. Thus droughts and floods are not only natural calamities, they are also man-made. Both are devastating in their nature and leave a trail of suffering, irreparable loss, misery, poverty and erosion of valuable soil.

In the plains and hills of the north, there is a mighty network of rivers and when they are in spate they cause devastation on a large scale. They destroy life and property as they burst their banks and dams. The worst affected people are those of poor and weaker sections of the society, as their small agricultural fields, huts and houses are destroyed and their means of subsistence devastated. But floods do not spare anyone, whether poor or wealthy. The scourge of floods is too severe for all to bear. In flood-affected areas standing crops, livestock, people, villages and towns are swept away. Houses, huts, bridges, rail-lines, and roads, etc. collapse like packs of cards. Power and electrical failures plunge entire regions in utter darkness. There is no drinking water, no food, no shelter during floods. And then there might be visitations of famine and epidemics, if proper remedial measures are not taken immediately. Had there been no droughts and floods, India would have been a very prosperous country, because it is mainly an agricultural country and more than 80% of its population depends on it, directly or indirectly.

Unfortunately for India, droughts and floods are an annual feature, and so far we have not been able to tame our mighty rivers and solve the problem of floods. During floods, a huge amount of funds and money is required to initiate relief and rescue measures. Relief camps with facilities for food, drinking water, and medicine, etc. are set up, liberal loans and subsidies are granted. Food supplies, etc. are also dropped for marooned people. They are rescued by boats and sometimes by helicopters. Many people lose their lives for want of quick, timely and effective rescue operations. The quick and proper disposal of dead bodies and carcasses also becomes a problem then.

To minimise the recurrence of floods certain firm, effective and proven steps should be taken. These measures can be divided into long-term and short-term ones. In the opinion of the experts, afforestation on a vast scale in the catchment areas and on flanks and slopes of the hills and mountains, is an effective measure to check floods. Plantation of trees on a mass scale in these areas will help check landslide, siltation of the river-beds and erosion of the soil, which are some of the main causes of floods. The destruction of forests, cutting of trees for timber and fuel is really suicidal. These should be effectively banned. Similarly, destruction of hills and mountains for stones and minerals, etc. should be immediately stopped. Afforestation and conservation of woods and green cover would go a long way in checking the overflow and siltation of the rivers. Erection of small irrigation dams and ponds at various points of advantage may also help in minimising the incidence of floods. Interlinking of rivers and waterways can prove another effective measure to tackle floods and deluge. It would help in taking excess of water to the regions where there is scarcity of rain and water. Moreover, construction of a series of small irrigation dams and reservoirs can help a lot in controlling the floods. They can also be used for power generation. A few of our rivers rise in Nepal and flow through Bangladesh. Therefore, the co-operation of these countries may be sought to check the floods. There are already some river projects undertaken jointly by India and Nepal but more co-operative efforts and understanding are needed in the areas of flood-control, afforestation, conservation and water storage for power-generation and irrigation. ●

10. INDIA IN THE 21ST CENTURY

WE have stepped into a new century. Talking about the future is always exciting. Man wants to peep into the future to find out what is in store for him and his fellow beings. Man's curiosity to know about the future and the shape of things and events to come has given rise to such subjects as astronomy, astrology, and palmistry, etc., which try to predict the events to come.

Now, what would be the future of India in the coming years of this century. Can we project and predict the future of India as a nation with some certainty and precision? Are we in a position to predict the conditions that are likely to prevail in future? How would the country look like, say after a decade? These are really very crucial questions. Should we expect a brave new world, full of peace, prosperity, hope, dynamism and health or a world congested, overpopulated, full of despair, selfishness, polluted and dominated by narrow, parochial and self-seeking politicians? Perhaps, we cannot answer these questions with the desired precision, accuracy and exactness. However, the subject is really thrilling, exciting and interesting. There is no harm in making a guess about the shape of events and things in the coming years.

Our late Prime Minister, Mr. Rajiv Gandhi often talked of taking India in to the 21st century. He was very optimistic and enthusiastic about the future of India and his faith and optimism were quite well founded. But, unfortunately, he was not destined to lead the country into the new century. He wanted to shape the destiny of India but did not know about his own tragic and untimely end. It sounds ironical, but in no way does it lessen his faith, hope, optimism and dynamism about the future of the country. Physically he is no more with us but his ideals, optimism, faith, enthusiasm and dynamism are with us. He symbolised the country's youth and bright future and continues to live in the form of young men and women of India. What is important is the spirit and it never dies.

Judging from the winds of change sweeping across, a fair and some sure future image of the country can easily be formed. In order to imagine the future image of the country, it is essential that we review the major trends, events and happenings in the past few decades, because future projections cannot be made correctly by ignoring present events and past happenings. The past, the present and the future present a logical time-sequence. They are like links of the same chain.

As a result of rapid and radical advancement in the fields of science, technology, medicine, and agriculture, many changes of far reaching significance have taken place during the last two-three decades. Atomic energy has been harnessed and space and time have been conquered to some extent. With the help of supersonic aeroplanes, the barrier of sound has been crossed, and now we can travel at tremendous speeds. Peoples and countries have come closer in terms of time and distance and the world looks like one big country, marked by pleasant diversities. Man has landed on the moon, and space laboratories have become a reality. The ominous clouds of the Cold War, threatening world peace and harmony, have receded. The wide use of computers and super-computers has revolutionised our life. In the field of entertainment, television and audio systems have transformed life completely. People have become better aware of issues like family planning, child and woman-welfare and have begun to accept the norm of a small, planned family. General awareness about ecology and environment is also on the increase. Many diseases, previously regarded as fatal, have now been controlled and eradicated, but diseases like cancer and AIDS have raised their ugly and deadly heads. On the basis of these developments, we look forward to a promising new era, with occasional gloom and despair.

In the coming years and decades, life in India will certainly be more convenient, comfortable and easy but real happiness and contentment will be more scarce. With the increased use of modern gadgets and devices, working, learning, communication and transportation will become easier, quicker, more comprehensive and less time-consuming. Man will become more and more materialistic, comfort-loving and competitive. Religion will be further pushed into the background and many of the present-day superstitions will be eliminated. People will have more leisure and spare time and so travelling and sight-seeing will become more popular. The coming years will bring greater industrial, economical, scientific and technological developments and India will be one of the leading lights in these areas. Consumerism will have a rapid growth and there will be many more new luxury items and consumer durables.

Many items, which are now considered a luxury, will not be so then as they will become ordinary things of daily domestic use. Farm technology will be further improved and food-production will increase. Consequently, there will be no shortage of food items, edible oils, vegetables and dairy products. Thus, there will be a marked improvement in the living standards of the people in general. They will be comparatively better off than they are at present. Many of the present towns will change into big cities and centres of trade and business.

As far as our population is concerned, it will perhaps surpass that of China in the coming years. At present, our population is over one billion, approximately one-sixth of the world population. Consequently, there will be pressure on our land, water and power resources. Housing and shelter will remain a serious problem. By the year 2020, metropolitan cities like Delhi, Mumbai, Kolkata and Chennai will become huge urban excrescence as a major portion of each of them will be covered by jhuggis and slums for want of adequate housing facilities. A few decades hence, India will emerge as a more powerful, strong, united and leading nation and, as such, will play a far more deciding and vital role in international affairs, specially in those of the U.N. and other world bodies. In the coming decades, secularism will prevail and people will become more tolerant, appreciative and broad-minded to one another's religious faiths and way of living. In the matter of marriage, sex and love, there will be increased liberal outlook and the gap between the two sexes will be further bridged. There will be more frequent cases of separation and divorce. The size of the family will be further reduced and the number of the old and the aged will rise rapidly. In the same proportion, the population of the children will decrease.

Secularism apart, India will remain religious at heart but much of religious observations and formalities will be casualities. The faith of the people will lead to further strengthening of the bonds of nationalism, national integration and unity. The problems of casteism, regionalism and communalism will be solved to a great extent, giving rise to better discipline, progress and a sense of patriotism. Gradually, the regional parties will be erased from the political scene of the country. The public will be more enlightened and aware about their political and social rights and duties and will exercise far more diligence in the exercise of their votes. People will be proud of being Indians in the real sense of the term and pseudo-patriots along with political gurus, will be exposed. In the coming decades, there will be more cohesiveness, uniformity, unity and integrity than now. The country may even have one civil code for all classes and communities in respect of marriage, etc.

These are some of the broad and rough outlines of the future. On the basis of scientific, technological, social, political and world developments that have taken place in the past, we can only guess. Finer details about what may happen, can be left for the future. The 21st century in itself is a very big period and the changes that will take place during these long years will be far more radical, fast, astonishing and unpredictable than those of the last century. Thus, only the coming decades will show the exact shape of things and events to come. There are thousands of things and possibilities which cannot be visualised at this point of time. One thing is certain. The future of our country is bright, hopeful, assuring and such as would inspire confidence, faith and optimism. But we must exert our best to make it doubly sure. Let us resolve to march ahead into the 21st century with confidence, fortitude, hope, courage and determination to face the new challenges of the new century. India as a nation has vast human and material resources at its command to scale new heights and establish new records in space technology, computer science, exploitation of non-conventional energy, the use of atomic energy for peaceful purposes, genetic engineering, bio-technology, micro-electronics and a host of other related fields of human activity. ●

11. UNITY OF INDIA

INDIA is an ancient country, a living example of stupendous paradoxes, extremes and their synthesis. Unity in diversity run through the entire fabric of the Indian society; its extraordinary heterogeneity strikes one and all with awe and wonder. People are left breathless and gaping at its sheer vastness, complexity and variety. India, the largest democracy in the world, is inhabited by one-sixth of mankind, occupying about a fortieth of the earth's surface. It is so fascinating and fantastic, with all its variety of colours, dresses, languages, dialects, religions, faiths, faces, races, customs, rites and cults. All these present a feast of colours of a panoramic scene painted on a huge, single piece of canvass, as it were. Notwithstanding all these apparent and endless diversities, India has always been one integrated whole as a nation, from Kashmir to Kanyakumari and from Dibrugarh to Dwarka.

India, the seventh largest country in the world, has a well defined geographical, cultural, political and social entity. It has been a meeting point and a melting pot of various cultures, civilisations, faiths and religions for centuries. It has outlived the test of time and aggressions. It is here that modernity and tradition, urban and rural, religion and secularism, spiritual and temporal, peaks and valleys embrace each other in counterbalance. It is so wonderful, fascinating, fantastic, mysterious, elusive and seemingly paradoxical that it baffles and defies description and analysis.

India is a land of great variety and its unique and ancient civilisation has been a great unifying factor. The vast number of diverse faiths, cults, beliefs, sects, religions, languages, manners, and lifestyles, etc. may confound a stranger, but in essence they represent the different aspects of one nation as do the petals of a lotus flower in bloom. These give you the same fascinating sweet fragrance, whether you take these petals severally and separately or collectively. This spirit of unity in diversity is very well enshrined in our Constitution, which says that it is the primary duty of every Indian citizen "to promote harmony and the spirit of common brotherhood amongst all the people of India, transcending religious, linguistic and regional or sectional diversities."

Tolerance and respect for all religions and faiths has been the hallmark of Indian civilisation. The religious life of India makes a complex but a wonderful pattern. Hinduism, which is not based on any single book or person, has the largest following. More than 80% of the population are Hindus. Hinduism is one of the most ancient and extant religions. It believes in oneness of the Universal Soul and is essentially monotheistic. It believes in the eternity of the soul and its reincarnations that eventually lead to final liberation and nirvana. This theory is based on the scientific principle of cause and effect.

Besides Hinduism, Christianity, Islam, Buddhism, Jainism, Sikhism have large following. Muslims in India form the largest religious minority and make India one of the largest Islamic nations. In fact, after Indonesia, India has the largest Muslim population in the world. The Christian Church in south India is much older than the coming of Islam in India. St. Thomas, one of the 12 disciples of Christ, was the first preacher of Christianity in India. He was a contemporary of St. Peter in Rome. Then, there are Parsis who came to India seeking refuge from religious persecution in Iran and brought Zoroastrianism. The Jews came quite early, about 2000 years ago. All these faiths and religions have been here, coexisting in harmony, peace and tolerance; and the communal clashes in recent decades may be considered as an exception.

Fundamentally, India is secular as a nation and yet profoundly spiritual and religious. The Indian Constitution guarantees all its citizens freedom of faith and worship. One can follow and preach any faith, religion and sect as long as it does not interfere in the religious freedom and rights of others. All are equal before law, without any discrimination of faith, cult, caste, creed, sex or language. India has always believed in freedom of thought, expression and faith. The people of this ancient nation have always been at liberty to pursue cultural, religious and spiritual goals of their own selection and choice. They have varied views and opinions on religion, political systems, economic order, and social problems, etc.

India is geographically, culturally and politically one, united and strong, and yet allows differences of thought, approach, religion and faith. It is this tolerance which has been a bench-mark of Indian culture and thought since times immemorial. India has an immense capacity and power to imbibe and absorb all good alien influences. If it didn't have this tolerance and power to assimilate foreign cultural influences, thought and philosophy would have been now extinct, as has been in the case of many ancient civilisations of the world. There has been useful interaction between the cultures of India and that of the other countries for the last several millennia. In the process, the Indian mind has assimilated much of the thoughts and conceptions of the cultures of other nations. Thus, India's contribution to world culture and civilisation has been immense. It has been the cradle of such great religions as Hinduism, Sikhism, Buddhism and Jainism.

But it is really regrettable that in recent years, particularly after 1947, so many ugly forces have raised their heads in the form of casteism, communalism, regionalism, and terrorism, etc. They pose a great threat and challenge to the unity, integrity, stability and progress of the country. These undesirable forces of evil, let loose by certain vested foreign powers, are hell bent on exploiting our spirit of tolerance, secularism, variety and diversity of faiths, religions, and languages, etc. But these nefarious designs of our enemies will never succeed. We are well aware of our responsibilities and duties as worthy citizens of this great ancient land and ready to fight tooth and nail to defeat these disruptive forces challenging our age-old solidarity and integrity. We shall definitely overcome, sooner rather than later, these fanatics, bigots and extremists trying to create communal tensions, religious intolerance and regional hatred at the instances of some hostile nations. We should identify such narrow, parochial, selfish and communal mischief makers and eliminate them for ever. Nobody can be allowed to encourage separatism, division, disharmony and disintegration. Some political parties are also to blame for it. They fight elections on the lines of caste, community, religion, region or language. They divide the people on communal basis, to use them as their vote banks in elections. These parties should be derecognised and their policies condemned in no uncertain terms. Unfortunately, some of the Indian political leaders are following in the footsteps of the British rulers who always adopted the policy of 'divide and rule'.

In spite of all these odds that have surfaced in recent years, India is one and united politically, culturally, geographically and socially. Our way of life, thinking, literature, heritage, customs and traditions are basically the same. The institutions of family and marriage are the same, so are our social and religious customs throughout the length and breadth of the country. Similarly, there are many fairs and festivals, etc., observed and enjoyed by the people of all communities and castes in common. All these facts and factors underline our cultural and emotional unity and integrity. ●

12. POVERTY ERADICATION

IT has been observed that India is a rich country inhabited by the poor. This paradoxical statement underlines the fact that India is very rich, both in material and human resources, which have not been properly used and exploited so far.

Poverty amidst plenty seems to be the main problem of India. The majority of our population lives in rural areas. But following the rapid growth in the number of large cities and towns, there has been migration from rural areas to these cities and urban industrial complexes on an unprecedented scale. It has not helped much in the alleviation of the rural poverty. Obviously, unless our efforts and planning are rural-oriented, nothing appreciable can be achieved. 'Go rural' should be our watchword.

Over 80% of the income of the rural poor is spent on food and the expenditure on shelter is also very high. The urban poor also spend almost the same proportion of their income on these two items. The remainder is too meagre to meet their demands of clothing, health, education, and entertainment, etc. The purchasing power of the Indian rural masses is miserably low. They are unable to afford even the basic needs of life. The problem of economic inequality and improper distribution of national income has been a chronic one. Consequently, the rich are becoming more rich and the poor more poor. The growth in industry and agriculture in the past few years has further encouraged concentration of wealth and resources in the hands of a few. What is needed are radical changes in our planning and implementation of schemes to remove all these inequalities, distortions and imbalances in the distribution of national income and resources. We must ensure land-reforms, self-reliance, quick redressal of the grievances of the weaker and vulnerable sections, like landless labourers, scheduled castes and tribes and the womenfolk. We should ensure that these weaker sections of the society are liberated from the vicious grip of the money-lenders, big farmers and landowners. Effective planning is the only way to eradicate poverty. There should be no faltering and hesitation in the implementation of our planning. Soon after our independence, we launched our Five Year Plans, which have yielded good dividends. Consequently, there has been self-sufficiency in foodgrains.

The Indian farmers are now ready to take risks because they are sure of speedier supply of agricultural inputs, modern irrigation facilities. quicker and easier loan and credit facilities by the government. And yet we cannot rest on our laurels. As far as pulses and oil-seeds are concerned, self-sufficiency is still to be achieved. Moreover, our population is growing very fast. The growth rate in food production has barely kept ahead of the growth of our population. The per capita availability of food grains in India has not risen appreciably. As far as fine and superior varieties of grains like wheat and rice are concerned, our achievements have been really laudable. But in coarse grains, like maize, barley, bajra, and jowar, etc., there has been no significant achievements. It only means that the interest of the poor masses have not been adequately served. They mostly consume coarse grains as their purchasing power is very low.

The Community Development Programme, started in 1952, should be further strengthened and expanded. This programme has helped significantly in development of villages. The scheme chiefly aims at providing more employment and production by the application of latest methods of agriculture, horticulture, animal husbandry, and fisheries, etc., and the establish-ment of subsidiary and cottage industries.

The whole country has been divided into a large number of community development blocks, with each one of these having about a 100 villages under it. Thousands of officials, administrators and gramsevaks have been engaged in the scheme. Consequently, there has been significant improvement but we still have a long way to go.

In a country like India, with a population of more than a billion people and a population growth rate of about 2.2%, the poverty eradication programme is bound to be arduous and long drawn. Over 35% of our population is estimated to be living below the poverty line, in spite of the fact that the main emphasis of our Five Year Plans has been on poverty eradication, modernisation of the economy and industry and self-reliance. For example, the main objectives of the Seventh Plan, beginning in 1985, were growth in food-grain production, increase in employment opportunities and rise in productivity. Obviously, our plans have to play a greater role as an instrument of growth and development in times to come. And this can be done only by greater and enlarged participation of the masses, especially in villages and small towns.

One of the main objectives of our Five Year Plans has been the expansion and creation of more employment opportunities in rural India. To achieve this objective, sufficient funds have been allocated under various employment schemes. For example, under the Jawahar Rozgar Yojna, the various states and Union Territories have been given funds in proportion to the number of people living below the line of poverty. Special consideration has been given to such areas as the hills, deserts and the islands under the scheme. Further, the devolution of funds to village panchayats is determined by the proportion of the scheduled castes and tribes and the backwardness of the region. The expenditure under this scheme is to be shared between the Centre and the states, in the ratio of 80 : 20. With the involvement of village panchayats in the scheme, wider participation of the rural people is envisaged. Jawahar Rozgar Yojana is the biggest of its kind in the world and a sum of Rs. 2,600 crore was earmarked by the Centre to implement it. The utilisation of funds is at the sole discretion of the gram and village panchayats and there will be no state intervention in the matter of selection of projects, etc. Based on decentralised planning, the scheme is bound to help thousands of families living below the poverty line in rural areas. It further shows that democracy is compatible with rural growth and development. In April 1999, a new scheme known as Swaranjayanti Gram Swarozgar Yojana was launched with a plan outlay of Rs. 1000 crore, to eradicate poverty and unemployment.

The economic reform process, now gathering momentum, will further help reduce poverty in villages and towns. The government's liberalisation policy has helped in rural employment because of the various incentives granted to the industries established in the backward and rural areas of the country. With industrial growth picking up, the picture will be still better. In the long term, the economic and industrial growth will increase the income of the poor substantially. Initially, the results of liberalisation and opening of the Indian economy may not be as appreciable as desired, in terms of poverty eradication and increase in employment for rural people, but ultimately it will result in reduction of poverty. It also ensures reduction in inequalities, because it has been found that distribution of national income and assets under a more open economy is less unequal. Privatisation will also help the government to devote its resources in a better manner to its social obligations

Therefore, the alleged contradiction between liberalisation, growth and social justice is unfounded. With liberalisation, India is bound to grow rapidly by virtue of its huge natural and human resources. The growth will be marked by improvement in standards of living, removal of poverty to a great extent and emergence of India as a great economic power. Thus, it is clear that eradication of poverty is intimately linked with the raising of productivity and employment, both in agricultural and industrial sectors. As removal of poverty, increase in employment and living standards of the people are our main priorities at this point of time, we shall have to strike a balance between the development of agriculture and industry. We cannot think of India without villages and agriculture. At the same time, industries cannot be asked to wait. Sometimes it is asked, should we give priority to agriculture over industry, or should industries get priority over agriculture? Perhaps both should go hand in hand in order to make India poverty-free, and an industrial major in the world. Food and agriculture are like the same sides of the coin while industries are the reverse. In the Indian context, both are ultimately interrelated and important. Items produced in mills and factories will be purchased by the masses only when they have enough money to buy them. And our masses in villages depend on agriculture for their livelihood and improvement in their living standards. Consumerism pre-supposes a sound agriculture base and income.

13. MASS COMMUNICATION IN INDIA

RADIO, T.V., films, newspapers, and periodicals, etc. are the various forms of the mass media and communication. The importance of these can hardly be overemphasised. They play a vital role in dissemination of knowledge and information, formation of public opinion, national integration and removal of superstition. The urgency and importance of multi-channels of mass communication for a country like India, with a population of more than a billion, is clear.

Radio broadcasting started in India in 1927, in Mumbai and Kolkata. Since then it has spread as a vast network, covering almost all the villages, hamlets, towns and cities. It was christened Akashwani in 1957. Now, there are over 100 stations of All India Radio, serving as very effective means of communication, education and entertainment. Radios and transistors are very popular as they are cheep, handy and affordable. Over 95% of our population is covered by its vast network of stations and broadcasting centres. Now there are about 273 bulletins for a duration of 37 hours in its regional, national and external services. It is one of the biggest news organisations of its kind in the world. There are 78 news bulletins in 19 languages in home service from Delhi alone.

Then there are 127 regional bulletins in 62 languages. In the external air service, bulletins in 67 languages and dialects are broadcast every day. Besides, there are sports bulletins, special bulletins, weather and Parliament bulletins. There are hosts of other, very useful bulletins, commentaries and broadcasts to cover events, people, news, and views of national and international importance. Yuva Vani is a programme for the youth of the nation, by the young men and women of the country, between the ages of 15 and 30. For school students most of the AIR stations have regular programmes, based on their school curriculum. Students of degree courses are also provided support and service on the air by many stations. Rural and agricultural programmes in various Indian languages and dialects are broadcast daily for the benefit of small and marginal farmers, agricultural labourers and others in the villages. Thus, radio in India has taken giant strides in these years.

Television came to India in 1959, with three days a week limited transmission. However, from 1965 these became regular. Since 1976 when Doordarshan came into being, it has emerged as a very powerful and effective means of mass communication. It has seen a phenomenal growth of installation of one transmitter a day in 1984 and after. A vast network of over 350 transmitters of the Doordarshan now reaches an estimated 80% of our population. The popularity of television is on the increase and soon it will cover the entire population of our country. In order to cater to the wide interests of large sections of our population, more channels are being added and introduced. The introduction of the Metro channel in 1984 in Mumbai, Kolkata and Chennai has been historical. Now, it is available in many cities and towns. The services of Doordarshan for school and university education have helped a lot in the promotion of education and training.

The satellite communication has really revolutionised the means of mass communication and information. The radio and television broadcasts via satellites have made communication instant and universal. It has turned the whole world into a global village. Now viewers have access to more and greater selection of viewing on T.V. The implications of satellite communication are really very complex, varied and far-reaching. It has its own inherent strengths and weaknesses, which are unfolding with the passage of time. But it is beyond any shadow of doubt that satellite communication will go a long way in helping a developing country like India in overcoming its many socio-economic problems and in the achievement of development goals.

The influence of films on Indian masses, as a means of mass communication, has been vast and abiding. The popularity of films is unquestionable. Hundreds of feature films and documentaries are made every year in India. Our film industry is one of the biggest in the world. In spite of its commercialism, its appeal and popularity is vast, abiding and immediate. It has tremendous possibilities but we should see to it that its box office aspects are not allowed to run riot. The Indian film industry should not forget its social and moral obligations. The industry should be precise, clear and sure about its scope, purpose and objectives. Similarly, the government should have no adhocism in respect to its policy in regard to the control, purpose and regulation of the industry. The multiplicity of authorities, which have a say in the industry, should be removed so as to provide healthy growth to the film industry. Moreover, censorship should be more liberal in its approach to films produced and screened. But film-makers should avoid too much sex and violence in their films. They should aim at healthy entertainment and desirable social and cultural change through this popular means of communication.

Freedom of speech and expression is very significant in a democracy. It includes the freedom of the films, the press, and broadcasting, etc. In other words, freedom of speech and expression means autonomy of the media. But autonomy also involves greater accountability. It means that there should be no loss of credibility. But commercialisation of mass media without proper safeguards can be dangerous. There is a lot of money in different media and there is the possibility of misuse of the media for personal gains. Autonomy of mass media is desirable but it is also desirable that it is self-regulatory and self-disciplined so as not to come into pressures and that it fulfils its commitments to values and ideals enshrined in our Constitution. Rights and duties go together. No autonomy, more specifically that of media, can have desirable objectives until and unless there are proper checks and balances to prevent its abuse. Therefore, it is essential that before granting autonomy to the electronic mass media, all its aspects are taken into consideration. In this context, the Prasar Bharti Bill 1989 comes to mind. It has tried to analyse different aspects of the matter in detail.

The Supreme Court judgement asking the Central Government to establish an independent public authority to control and regulate the use of electronic media is a welcome decision. It implies that freedom of speech applies not just to the print but also to the electronic media. This judgement marks a new, bold and significant beginning in liberating electronic media from government control and monopoly. ●

14. TERRORISM IN INDIA

TERRORISM is global. In recent decades, it has acquired new dimensions and there seems no end to it. The way it has grown and spread beyond limits during the last few years, is a matter of great concern for all of us. Though it has been condemned and denounced by leaders in international forums, it is increasing by leaps and bounds and is in evidence everywhere. The trigger-happy terrorists and extremists use all sorts of weapons and strategies to terrorise their adversaries. They explode bombs, use rifles, hand-grenades, rockets, ransack houses, loot banks and establish-ments, destroy religious places, kidnap people, highjack buses and planes, indulge in arson and rape and do not spare even children.

Consequently, the world is becoming a totally unsafe, insecure, dangerous and fearful place day by day. This ruthless chain of action and reaction, full of horrifying violence, is much too dangerous to be ignored or taken lightly. Terrorism, violence, bloodshed, and killings, etc. have become the order of the day. India, Pakistan, the whole of the Middle East, Afghanistan, parts of Europe, Latin America, and Sri Lanka, etc. all seem to be in the grip of this many-headed monster.

Terrorists aim at achieving political power by overthrowing and destroying the democratic and lawful governments. They try to create disturbance and unstable conditions on a vast scale to achieve their own political ends. They are trained, inspired and financed by very powerful national and international vested interests. They receive deadly weapons and ammunition from these powers and create havoc. This ugly and dangerous socio-political phenomenon called terrorism knows no limits of land, time, race, religion or creed. It is spread worldwide and is becoming more and more popular among the politically frustrated groups, religious fundamentalists and misled factions in the society. They indulge in all sorts of anti-social and anti-government activities to achieve their narrow, sectarian and unholy aims. Sometimes, the terrorists may have very good objectives but then they resort to violence as they are unable to participate in the democratic process because of their various inherent weaknesses.

Terrorism in India is not new, but it has increased very rapidly in the last few years. Terrorism in India should be looked upon as an integral part of our colonial legacy. The British followed the policy of 'divide and rule' and ultimately divided the subcontinent into two nations, which later grew into three after the independence of Bangladesh. Post-independence and post-partition violence and terrorism was unprecedented. This partition on the basis of religion, faith and community has sown seeds of hatred, violence, terrorism, separatism and communal divide and will continue growing and flowering for a long time.

The rise of extremism and terrorism in our north-eastern states of Nagaland, Mizoram, Tripura, Manipur and Assam, etc. is also part of our colonial legacy. The long colonial rule never attempted to bring the tribals of these states into the mainstream of the nation. Rather, a feeling of hatred, alienation and disharmony was created in their hearts. Consequently, they felt neglected after independence and could not take part in the democratic process of the country. They were misled by a false sense of losing their ethnic identity and independence, and decided to take to terrorism and violence. They were helped in their futile armed struggle by neighbouring countries, who never liked to see India as a united, powerful, and successful democracy. This emergence of terrorism in our north-eastern states also reflects the lack of will and proper efforts on the part of our political leaders and the government to bring these big groups of tribals into the national mainstream and the democratic process.

Besides socio-political and economic aspects, psychological, emotional and religious aspects are also involved in the problem. All these create strong feelings and extremism. The unprecedented spate of terrorism in the recent past in Punjab can be understood and appreciated only in this background. The demand for a separate Khalistan by these alienated sections of the society became so strong and powerful at one point in time that it put our unity and integrity under strain. But ultimately good sense prevailed, both on the government and the people, and electoral process was started in which the people participated wholeheartedly. This involvement of people in the democratic process, coupled with strong measures adopted by security forces, helped us wage a successful battle against terrorism in Punjab.

Terrorism, as a means to achieve socio-political aims in Punjab got much support from Pakistan by way of supply of arms and ammunition, training and finance. The people in power in Pakistan have always been hostile to India because of their own political compulsions. They have been trying their best to destabilise and disturb the society in India. They train and equip terrorists with arms and then smuggle them into the country. Poverty, unemployment, and lack of education, etc. among the people further worsen the situation. Under various political, communal and economical pressures, they succumb to the temptations and discard the democratic process, finding it unsuitable for improving their miserable lot. Terrorism in Jammu and Kashmir is of this nature. Widespread poverty, unemployment, neglect of youth, peasants and working class and emotional alienation are some of the main reasons of extremism in the province. The hostile forces across our borders are also helping it a lot. The emergence of Bangladesh as an independent state with India's help was too much for Pakistan to tolerate. Smarting under this humiliation, the leaders of Pakistan spare no pains to destabilise and disturb peace in the Indian sub-continent.

The series of bomb-blasts in Mumbai and other cities of India were planned in Pakistan and executed with their financial help. Pakistan-sponsored terrorism in Jammu and Kashmir has caused deaths of thousands of people, including innocent civilians, defence and security personnel during the last five years. It has also caused loss of property worth several crores of rupees in the state. In spite of loud and vociferous denouncement of terrorism and extremism in various international forums by the Pakistan government, militants, fundamentalist and terrorists are being trained there in secret and well-established camps run by the ISI and other such groups and agencies. These extremists have found a very safe sanctuary there. It has been established beyond any shadow of doubt that Pakistan-trained militants and extremists had their hand in the 2001 crash of the U.S. World Trade Centre in New York. Such activities certainly boomerang and now Pakistan finds itself in the grip of terrorism. During the year 2002, over one thousand people have been killed in terrorist activities in the city of Karachi alone. The communal, fundamentalist and sectarian clashes, violence and militancy among the Mohajirs, Sunnis, Shias and other such groups is now very common there. The roots of organised and large scale terrorism and violence in Pakistan are quite deep and widespread.

Terrorism is a global problem and as such it cannot be solved in isolation. What is needed is international co-operative efforts to fight against this global menace. All the governments of the world should simultaneously and continuously crack down on militants and terrorists. The global menace can be reduced and eliminated only by close co-operation between various countries. The countries from where militancy springs should be clearly identified and declared as terrorist states. It is very difficult for any terrorist activity to thrive for long in a country unless there is strong external support to it. Terrorism achieves nothing, solves nothing and the quicker this is understood, the better. It is sheer madness and an exercise in futility. In terrorism there cannot be a victor or vanquished. If terrorism becomes a way of life, the leaders and heads of states of the various countries alone are to blame. This vicious circle is their own creation and only their combined and pooled efforts can check it. Terrorism is a crime against humanity and should be dealt with an iron hand and the forces behind it should be exposed. Terrorism adversely affects the quality of life and hardens attitudes.

In the ultimate analysis, all terrorist groups are criminal. They do no distinguish between good and evil, neither do they spare anybody, not even women and children. For example, Jaish-e-Mohammed, a terrorist outfit active in Kashmir, has been most ruthless and rapacious. It began as a support organisation for Afghan Mujahideen in the beginning of 1980s. It is now operating worldwide under different names. Their professed aim is to establish Islam throughout the world, through jehad. They train their cadres in making bombs, explosives, hurling grenades and using light and heavy weapons. They have a large number of hideouts in the valley of Kashmir. The man who made the bomb that blew off the New York World Trade Centre, belonged to this group. They find the whole world, including India, a fair game for their terrorist acts.

●

15. WOMEN IN INDIA

SINCE independence there has been much improvement in the lot of women in India. They enjoy perfect equality with men. They have all the rights and privileges possessed by the males. Our Constitution guarantees them all those rights, freedom, and privileges enjoyed by the male. Consequently, they now feel emancipated and free. The women of India, who form almost 50% of the population, have equal opportunities and rights and can aspire to any position and status in society. Many of them are in top positions in various fields of life. A few of them have been great political leaders, entrepreneurs, administrators and business persons. This marked change in their outlook, social and economic status reflects the fact that their emancipation has been almost complete. It is a fact that Indian women have much better status than their counterparts in many other developing countries.

Today, women in India are well conscious of their rights and privileges and they are politically, socially, economically and educationally not backward anymore. Their participation in the democratic process and elections has been quite impressive. In a large number of constituencies women voters outnumber men voters on the days of polling. They are contesting elections at various levels in far greater numbers. Their political wisdom and social sagacity has now been fully recognised. The status of women in India in modern times has undergone a sea change. During the last few decades, India has produced many great women leaders, social workers, administrators, reformers and literary personalities like Annie Besant, Vijaya Lakshmi Pandit, Sucheta Kripalani, Indira Gandhi, P.T. Usha, Raj Kumari Amrit Kaur, Padmaja Naidu, Kalpana Chawla, Mother Teresa, Mahadevi Verma, Subhadra Kumari Chauhan, and Amrita Pritam, etc. India really feels very proud because of these great women and their great achievements in various fields. Their contribution in the fields of art, science, and sports, etc. has also been equally significant and memorable. Their active participation in various social, political, economical, educational, scientific and other nation-building activities as mothers, wives, sisters and daughters has been of vital importance in taking the country to greater heights. And yet, there is no room for any complacency. They are doubly burdened as they have to work hard, both as employed women and housewives. Ours is still a male-dominated society and women have to depend on men for protection and help at every stage of life. As a daughter, she needs protection from her father; as a married woman, she has to depend on her husband; and, in old age again, she has to depend upon her husband or son.

Women in India are still exploited and abused. They are still regarded as inferior to men. The birth of a female child is considered a curse in parts of the country. Daughters are considered a liability because of many social evils like dowry, etc. In spite of full legal and Constitutional protection, in practice, women are still much exploited and abused. Their condition in villages is far worse. They are not aware at all about their rights and privileges and fully depend on men. Even very highly educated and gainfully employed women in urban India cannot spend their earnings as they like. The strings of their purses are controlled by their menfolk. This unhealthy attitude of men towards women, with regard to their privilege to spend their hard earned money, has been a source of much tension in the families. Thus, in our tradition-oriented society male dominance still prevails. A husband has a far superior position over his wife and all major decisions are taken by him without taking into consideration her wishes and aspirations. This has created an imbalance and disharmony in the families. There has been appreciable change in our attitude as far as the employment of women is concerned. We do like that our wives, daughters or sisters are gainfully employed but as far as their right to spend their earnings is concerned, our attitude is still unchanged and conservative. A working woman helps her husband by bringing additional income, but as a housewife she has no help from her husband. Men regard household chores below their dignity and never help women in their work. Thus, women are doubly burdened, which often causes tension, maladjustment and family problems.

There is much to be done towards emancipation of women in India. They are still subdued and dominated by men and cannot assert their equality as desired in every walk of life. In a number of our states, the custom of child marriage still exists, widow remarriage is not allowed, and girls are still given away in marriages against their will. Then there is the dowry system. Poor parents cannot afford to give dowry and so are obliged either to keep their daughters unmarried or give them away in marriages to unmatched husbands. Women, specially in rural India, still find themselves weak, helpless and exploited. The rate of literacy among them is alarmingly low. Sometimes they are treated no better than commodities. They are still confined to the four walls of their house, engaged in household drudgery. They have been forced by arrogant men to play a totally subordinate role because they are economically and socially not independent. This has been further helped by our old, outdated and conservative customs. Their hard work and toil as housewives and working women, though significant enough to run a household and family, still goes unrewarded and unrecognised.

The present status of women in India has to be further consolidated and improved. It cannot be achieved unless women themselves come forward and organise themselves as a power to be reckoned with. They should stop thinking in terms of being the weaker sex. They should rise as one powerful body and fight the menace of dowry and child-marriage. They should fight tooth and nail wherever there is abuse, exploitation, humiliation and injustice. They should raise their voices against all social evils and male arrogance. They should wage a relentless war against "apartheid of sex". They should come forward and take more active part in the political affairs of the country and get themselves elected in greater numbers to public offices. Their representation in our various legislatures is still too meagre. Unless the women of India organise their own movements in a powerful manner they will be left out of taking vital decisions. They should assert and achieve economic independence so as to be able to play their proper and legitimate role in society.

Indian women are intelligent, hard-working, courageous and full of love, and compassion. With these qualities of head and heart they are quite competent in breaking all the bondage that binds them in traditional subordination and slavery. Endowed with the qualities of beauty, love, strength, tolerance, sacrifice, and creativity, etc. they can do wonders for themselves and for others. In the present day India, they can further consolidate their position and redefine their relationship with men, based on equality and mutual respect by using their strengths more wisely. It is of no use to curse and bemoan their fate as the weaker sex. They should unite and struggle against injustice, discrimination, ill-treatment, abuse and exploitation. Much really depends on women themselves. The future of women in India seems bright but it is women themselves who can ensure it by being vigilant, alert and united. They will have to raise their voices against any violation of their rights and privileges. It is said that God helps those who help themselves and it is equally true in the case of the equality and liberty of women in India. ●

16. DEMOCRACY IN INDIA

ABRAHAM Lincoln, the 16th President of the United States of America, aptly defined democracy as a government of the people, by the people and for the people. This definition clearly underlines the basic tenet that, in this form of government, people are supreme. The ultimate power is in their hands and they exercise it in the form of electing their representatives at the time of elections. In modern times this type of democracy, which is representative in nature, is most suitable. The other type, the direct democracy in which the people themselves enact and implement laws and run the administration, is now not feasible as countries are large and their populations huge. In a country like Switzerland, which has comparatively small population, direct democracy can still be found.

India is the biggest democracy in the world, with a population of over one billion. India, a union of states, is a sovereign socialist, secular, democratic, republic, with a parliamentary system of government. The republic is governed in terms of the Constitution, which was adopted on 26 November, 1949 and came into force on 26 January, 1950. During the past fifty-three years there have been regular elections to the Parliament and state legislatures. This reflects the maturity and wisdom of the Indian electorate, in whom the ultimate power and sovereignty rests. With the passage of time, Indian voters have become more assertive and active as regards their participation in the process of democracy. The turnout of Indian voters has significantly increased during the past elections. It was about 52% only during the Lok Sabha elections of 1952 which increased to 64% during the ninth Lok Sabha elections held in 1989. Similarly during the last elections for Parliament, the voters turnout has been quite encouraging. This phenomenon reflects the growing political awareness and maturity of the Indian masses, which, in turn, has made the various political parties more conscious of their responsibility and accountability to the people.

Indian democracy has been quite successful and its future seems quite bright. The Indian voters have exercised their right to vote fearlessly and judiciously. Free, fair and fearless elections is one of the basic pre-conditions for the success of democracy. The Election Commission, which is a Constitutional authority, is responsible for conducting the elections. It is headed by the Chief Election Commissioner, whose independence is sought to be preserved and protected by a special Constitutional provision, to the effect that he cannot be removed from his office, except in like manner, and on like grounds, as a judge of the Supreme Court.

Indian democracy has very deep and strong foundations. The credit for this strong democratic foundation rightly belongs to our leaders like Mahatma Gandhi, Dr. Rajendra Prasad, Pt. Jawahar Lal Nehru, Lal Bahadur Shastri and Indira Gandhi, etc. Their contributions to the success of Indian democracy have been immeasurable.

Indian democracy is based on adult franchise and a healthy and competitive party-system. There are a number of national and regional political parties, like Indian National Congress, Bhartiya Janata Party, Janata Dal, C.P.I., Bahujan Samaj Party, C.P.M., Samajvadi Party, Telugu Desam, Muslim League, Shiv Sena, Kerala Congress, National Conference, and Akali Dal, etc. These parties play a significant role in the elections and in the smooth functioning of the democracy. These political parties are the very life-blood of Indian democracy. The political parties, in opposition to the government, exercise certain checks in the form of criticism of the government so as to ensure that it does not degenerate into dictatorship and a rule of the few. They criticise the government policies in a democratic and constructive spirit so that national integration, secularism, unity, liberty, and the rights of the people, etc. are preserved and further strengthened. They help in the formation of public opinion as well. Thus, political parties see that there is nothing against the spirit of democracy, freedom, equality and social justice. In the absence of political parties, we cannot think of smooth and effective functioning of a democracy. Different political parties may have different ideologies but they all aim at the good of the people and the country. The party system in India has been a great factor in giving meaning and life to democracy. With the passage of time, a new and healthy relationship has developed between the ruling party and the opposition parties on the one hand and between the public and the political parties on the other. It is because of the enlightened Indian voters and political parties in opposition that the government and the party in power have been more responsive and accountable to the people and their representatives. Obviously, democracy is not a one-sided game and it needs two or more players in the form of ruling party, parties in opposition and the electorate.

Liberty, equality, justice and fraternity are the very cornerstones of democracy. They are not available under dictatorship and utilitarian forms of government. Without freedom of speech, expression of faith, profession, and association, etc. democracy is meaningless. Similarly, right to own property is one of the fundamental rights under democracy. The Indian Constitution offers all the Indian citizens, individually and collectively, these basic freedoms and rights. They are guaranteed in the Constitution in the form of six broad categories of Fundamental Rights and are justifiable. It means that each and every Indian citizen has the right to Constitutional remedies for the enforcement of these rights. There is free, independent and separate judiciary to see that these rights are not violated and tampered with. All are equal before law, right from the Prime Minister to a peon. This is the very spirit and essence of our democracy. An independent, strong and incorruptible judiciary is one of the main pillars of democracy.

The spirit of democracy in India is deep-rooted and all-pervading. It has stood the test of time all these years and faced many challenges. It is strong enough to face new challenges. India's destiny as a nation depends on how successfully our democratic system will work in the years to come. Still there are many serious challenges before our democracy. Communalism, separatism, casteism, terrorism, mobocracy, and illiteracy, etc. are some of the basic problems and challenges being faced by the Indian democracy. Ours is a secular country but, at times, communal and fundamentalist forces raise their ugly heads and cause considerable strain and threat to the spirit of democracy. Therefore, we have to be very vigilant and alert about it. Secularism means freedom to profess, practice and propagate one's religion without interfering with that of others. There cannot be any discrimination on the basis of one's faith and religion either. There is no state religion and all religions and sects are equal before the law. Democracy has been successful in India because we are a tolerant people and have proper regard for the others' point of view. Difference of opinion is not only compatible with democracy, but an essential ingredient for it.

Indian voters are mature and wise and well aware of their responsibility as citizens of a democratic country. They have never failed to rise to the occasion whenever the spirit of democracy has been in danger. For example, soon after the imposition of Emergency in June 1975, when general elections were held in March 1977, the voters decisively voted against the ruling party led by Mrs. Indira Gandhi and installed Janata Party's government in the Centre. It was for the first time that the Indian National Congress was routed because of the imposition of Emergency, during which the spirit of democracy underwent a shocking and traumatic experience. Thus, the foundations of Indian democracy are well-laid and strong. The various challenges and threats faced by it have further strengthened its spirit. The fair and free elections, independent judiciary, enlightened voters, nationalistic political parties and fundamental rights guaranteed by Constitution ensure a bright future for Indian democracy, notwithstanding the various strains, stresses, threats and challenges posed by forces hostile to the spirit of democracy. ●

17. PANCHAYATI RAJ

THE panchayat system in India goes back to the Vedic times. It has been an integral part of a self-contained and self-sufficient rural administration. A panchayat consisted of five or more public representatives, selected or elected by the people. A panch could be removed if people so liked. The panchayat was headed by a Sarpancha or a Chief Sarpancha, who presided over the meetings and deliberations of a panchayat. This council of panchas was fully responsible for the administration and development of a village. These five or more officials, constituting a panchayat, represented all the major sections of rural society. They administered justice, ruled over disputes, punished the guilty and looked after the welfare of the people. It functioned as a very important administrative body at various levels of villages, districts and provinces. These panchayats or local bodies also looked after the temples, hospitals, welfare of the poor and other charitable works like digging and maintenance of ponds, wells, and the irrigation system, etc.

With the centralisation of power, village panchayats came to be neglected, ensuring the rights and privileges of the ruling classes, nobility and feudal community only. These people concentrated powers in their own hands with the help of the state. This gave rise to authoritarianism, tyranny and exploitation of the rural poor, landless, and marginal farmers.

The reincarnation of Panchayati Raj, as a system of local self-government administered by a council or 'Panchayat' duly elected in a free and fair manner, is a step in the right direction. It is in keeping with the very spirit of democracy. It is essential that, to strengthen democracy, the panchayat system in India be given all possible help and encouragement. It will further help decentralisation of power and check the degeneration of democracy in a very effective manner. It has been an established fact that authoritarianism and too much concentration of power are the main obstacles in the process of democracy, which stands for full participation of the masses in the administration through regular fair and free elections, etc. The Panchayati Raj system has been purposefully and specially designed to take care of various rural problems. It provides the administrative and legislative apparatus for implementation of the programmes of rural development. The 64th Constitution Amendment Bill of May 15, 1989 has been a landmark in this context. It gave a new lease of life to Panchayati Raj as a truly representative system in our country. During the debate on the subject, the then Prime Minister Rajiv Gandhi told the Lok Sabha that "Too often in the past Panchayati Raj has had functions without finances, responsibilities without authority, duties without the means for carrying them out. The Bill seeks to remove these disparities and bottlenecks and to make these rural legislatures or councils a fit and effective instrument of self-government." The Bill also made it obligatory that elections be held regularly every five years, but various states have failed to fulfil this obligation and the Centre has had to intervene. Thus, the Bill has proved a milestone in revitalising an ancient and time-tested democratic institution.

The Panchayati Raj system is best suited for developmental and administrative requirements of rural population and society because of wide variation in the nature of local problems. It is an inexpensive form of local self-government, which can suitably identify the local problems and issues, particularly of the poor and weaker sections of society, like scheduled castes, scheduled tribes, small, marginal and landless farmers, women and backward classes. It also ensures quick and equitable measures to solve the problems. It provides a proper forum, where local people can meet, discuss and chalk out programmes, policies and their speedy implementation. It also ensures decentralisation of power, and effective developmental activities, in which active participation of the rural masses can be envisaged.

The main objective of the system is to develop a method of decentralisation and devaluation of powers, functions and authority to the rural folk with a view to ensure rapid socio-economic progress and speedier and inexpensive justice. This is to be achieved through increasing agricultural production, development of cottage and rural industries, fuller and proper utilisation of available local, natural and human resources with the active participation of the people. Besides progressive decentralisation of powers and authority, it aims at improving the living standard of the rural people in general and the weaker sections in particular.

It has a three-tier structure that includes Village Panchayats, Panchayat Samitis and the Zila Parishads. While in most of the states there is a three-tier structure, in some states and Union Territories there is only a two-tier system and in some cases only one-tier structure. The village or Gram Panchayat functions at the village level. Each village has its own panchayat. In case of very small villages, there can be a common panchayat for a group of villages. The Gram Sabha or the Village Council, consisting of all the adult members of the village, elect the members of the panchayat. These members elect their chairman or head, known as Pradhan. They hold the office of the Gram Panchayat normally for a period of three years. Every panchayat has its own secretary and a Gramsevak to help it in its various functions. The panchayat chalks out the programme for agricultural production and co-operative management of the land. It also seeks to ensure a minimum standard of cultivation for raising agricultural production.

Panchayat Samitis work at the block level. These main executive bodies have all the elected Village Pradhans of the

Gram Panchayats as their members. The Presidents and Vice Presidents of these Samitis are elected from among these members for a period of three years. The main function of the Panchayat Samiti is to prepare, execute and co-ordinate the developmental programme at the block level. It is responsible for preparing and implementing plans for the development of agriculture, animal husbandry, fisheries, cottage and small scale industries, rural health by the block development officer and extension officers.

Then there are Zila Parishads. These function at the district level and are responsible for making, executing and co-ordinating the programmes of rural development for the entire district. A Zila Parishad has the presidents of the Panchayat Samitis in the district, the members of the legislative assembly (MLAs) from the district and the members of the Parliament (MPs) representing the district as its members. All these members elect their Chairman, from amongst themselves. The district collector and other government officials provide guidance and help for formation and implementation of development schemes and programmes.

Thus, the panchayat system in India assumes a very significant role because nearly 80% of its population lives in villages, spread over about 95% of its geographical area. This system is quite rational, practicable and in perfect harmony with the spirit of democracy and should be further strengthened and encouraged. It should be made economically viable and self-sufficient by providing adequate resources, funds and generous grants. The reservation of seats for women, scheduled castes and tribes in panchayats is a welcome step, for it would make the institution of panchayat more democratic, representative and balanced. The panchayat elections are conducted and supervised by the Election Commission to ensure free and fair elections. All these measures ensure a bright and long lasting future of panchayat system in India.

18. HUMAN RIGHTS

THE right to live and exist, the right to equality, including equality before law, non-discrimination on grounds of religion, race, caste, sex or place of birth, and equality of opportunity in matters of employment, the right to freedom of speech and expression, assembly, association, movement, residence, the right to practice any profession or occupation, the right against exploitation, prohibiting all forms of forced labour, child labour and trafficking in human beings, the right to freedom of conscience, practice and propagation of religion and the right to legal remedies for enforcement of the above are basic human rights. These rights and freedoms are the very foundations of democracy. Obviously, in a democracy the maximum number of the freedoms and the rights are enjoyed by the people. Besides these are political rights, which include the right to contest an election and to vote freely for a candidate of one's choice. Human rights are a benchmark of a developed and civilised society. But rights cannot exist in a vacuum. They have their corresponding duties. Rights and duties are the two aspects of the same coin. Liberty never means licence. Rights pre-suppose a rule of law, where each and everyone in the society follows a code of conduct and behaviour for the good of all. It is the sense of duty and tolerance that gives meaning to rights. Rights have their basis in the principle of live and let live. For example, my right to speech and expression involves my duty to allow others to enjoy the same freedom of speech and expression. Rights and duties are inextricably interlinked and interdependent. A perfect balance is to be maintained between the two. Whenever there is imbalance, there is chaos. A sense of tolerance, propriety and adjustment is a must for enjoyment of rights and freedom. Human life sans basic freedom and rights is meaningless. Freedom is the most precious possession without which life would become intolerable, a mere abject and slavish existence. In this context the famous and oft-quoted lines of Milton from his *Paradise Lost* come to mind : "To reign is worth ambition though in hell/Better to reign in hell, than serve in heaven."

But then liberty cannot survive without its corresponding obligations and duties. An individual is a part of society in which he enjoys certain rights and freedom only because of fulfilment of certain duties and obligations towards others. Thus, freedom is based on mutual respect for each other's rights. A fine balance is to be maintained between the two or there will be anarchy and bloodshed. The human rights can best be preserved and protected in a society steeped in morality, discipline and social order.

Violation of human rights is most common in totalitarian and despotic states. In the theocratic states there is much persecution and violation in the name of religion and the minorities suffer the most. Even in democracies, violation and infringement of human rights and freedom is widespread. The women, children and the weaker sections of the society are victims of these transgressions and violence. The U.N. Commission on Human Rights' main concern is to protect and promote human rights and freedom in the nations of the world. In its various sessions held from time to time in Geneva, it adopts various measures to encourage world-wide observations of these basic human rights and freedom. It calls on its member states to furnish information regarding measures complied with the Universal Declaration of Human Rights whenever there is a complaint of violation of these rights. It reviews human rights situations in various countries of the world and initiates remedial measures when required. It was much concerned and dismayed at the apartheid being practised in the South Africa till recently. The Secretary General then declared, "The United Nations cannot tolerate apartheid. It is a legalised system of racial discrimination, violating the most basic human rights in South Africa. It contravenes the letter and spirit of the United Nations Charter. That is why over the last forty years, my predecessors and I have urged the Government of South Africa to dismantle it." Now, although apartheid is no longer practised in that country, there are other forms of apartheid being blatantly practiced worldwide. For example, sex-apartheid is most rampant. Women are subject to abuse and exploitation. They are not treated equally, they are paid less than their male counterparts for the same kind of jobs. In employment, promotions, and possession of property, etc., they are most discriminated against. Similarly, the rights of children are not observed properly. They are abused and exploited. They are forced to work hard in very dangerous situations. They are sexually assaulted and exploited, sold and bonded for labour.

The Commission has found that religious persecution, torture, summary executions without judicial trials, intolerance, slavery-like practices, kidnapping, and political disappearance, etc., are being practised even in the so-called advanced countries and societies. The continued acts of extreme violence, terrorism and extremism in various parts of the world like, Pakistan, India, Iraq, Afghanistan, Israel, Somalia, Algeria, Lebanon, Chile, China, and Myanmar, etc., by the governments, terrorists, religious fundamentalists, and mafia outfits, etc., is a matter of grave concern for the entire human race. Violation of freedom and rights by terrorist groups backed by states is one of the most difficult problems being faced by the society. For example, Pakistan has been openly collaborating with various terrorist groups, indulging in extreme violence in India and other countries. In this regard the U.N. Human Rights Commission in Geneva adopted a significant resolution, which was co-sponsored by India, focussing on gross violation of human rights perpetrated by terrorist groups backed by some states. The resolution expressed its solidarity with the victims of terrorism and proposed that a U.N. Fund for victims of terrorism be established soon. The Indian delegation on this occasion recalled that, according to the Vienna Declaration also, terrorism is nothing but the destruction of human rights for it shows total disregard for the lives of innocent men, women and children. The delegation further argued that terrorism cannot be treated as a mere crime because it is systematic and widespread in its killing of civilians. Violation of human rights, whether by states, terrorists, separatist groups, armed fundamentalists or extremists, is condemnable. Regardless of the motivation, such acts should be condemned categorically in all forms and manifestations, wherever and by whomever they are committed, as acts of aggression aimed at the destruction of human rights, fundamental freedom and democracy. The Indian delegation also underlined concerns about the growing connection between terrorist groups as well as the consequent commission of serious crimes, including rape, torture, arson, looting, murder, kidnappings, blasts, and extortions, etc.

Violation of human rights and freedom gives rise to alienation, dissatisfaction, frustration and acts of terrorism. The governments run by very ambitious and self-seeking people often use repressive measures and find violence and terror as an effective means of control. But state terrorism, violence and transgression of human freedom is a very dangerous strategy. This has been the background of all revolutions in the world. Whenever there is systematic and widespread state persecution and violation of human rights, rebellion and revolution have taken place. The French, American, Russian and Chinese Revolutions are glowing examples of human history. The first war of India's Independence in 1857 was a result of a long and systematic oppression of the Indian masses. The rapidly increasing discontent, frustration and alienation with the British rule gave rise to strong national feelings and demand for political privileges and rights. Ultimately the Indian people, under the leadership of Mahatma Gandhi, made the British to leave India, setting the country free and independent.

The human rights and freedom ought to be preserved at all cost. Their curtailment degrades human life. Human rights may be reshaped according to the political needs of the country but they should not be distorted out of shape. Tyranny and regimentation, etc., are inimical of humanity and should be resisted effectively and unitedly. The sanctity of human values, freedom and rights must be preserved and protected. Human Rights Commissions should be established in all the countries to take care of human freedom and rights. In cases of violation of human rights, affected individuals should be properly compensated and it should be ensured that these do not take place in future. These commissions can become effective instruments in percolating the sensitivity to human rights down to the lowest levels of the governments and administrations. The formation of National Humans Rights Commission in October 1993 in India is really commendable and should be followed by other countries. ●

19. TOURISM IN INDIA

The Taj Mahal, Agra, India

TOURISM in India is now recognised as an industry generating huge business and employment. With the opening up of the economy and the globalisation of business, tourism is likely to provide further impetus to economic modernisation in the country. It promotes national integration and unity, creates employment opportunities and increases foreign exchange earnings. It also encourages handicrafts and cultural activities. Travel and tourism have great educational, cultural, entertainment, national, international and business value. Travel has always been a new, refreshing, exciting and rewarding experience, both for domestic and foreign travellers.

India with its vast cultural, historical, scenic, artistic and natural wealth has great potential. There are numerous historical places, monuments, pilgrimage centres, shrines, temples, wildlife sanctuaries, hill stations, sea-resorts, places of winter sports and ancient and modern cities steeped in glory and fascination. Besides, its diversity of cultures, religions, languages, dresses, and weather conditions, etc. add more colour to tourism and travel. Consequently, international tourism in India has grown substantially during the last four decades. The foreign tourist arrivals in the country has registered a growth of about 15%. It has today become one of the highest net foreign exchange earning sectors. It is expected to account for increased percentage of the gross domestic product (GDP) in the coming years. During 2000–2001, the country earned nearly Rs. 15,000 crore in foreign exchange through this sector.

Domestic tourism plays a vital role in achieving various objectives of national unity, integration, cultural harmony, social tolerance and cohesion. The fast means of travel and communication have brought the distant places of tourist interest in the country closer than ever before. This has resulted in a keen desire in people to travel to different parts of the land and to have first-hand knowledge of them. With the rapid improvement in the living standards, and the increase in the income of the middle classes, the potential for domestic tourism has grown substantially during these years. With a view to diversify tourist attractions, development of beach and hill-resorts has been taken up and infrastructural facilities have been strengthened. In order to increase these facilities, the central Department of Tourism is trying its best to help the various states and union territories with liberal financial aid, etc. More and more Yatri Niwas hotels, tourist lodges, wayside inns, restaurants, cafeterias, tourist bungalows, hotels, and motels, etc., are being opened both in public and private sectors. In addition, financial assistance is being extended by the Centre to state governments for adventure sports activities, tourist transport, and tented accommodation, etc. To consolidate the development of tourism infrastructure, it has been decided to intensively develop a few selected areas/circuits. Seventeen such areas/circuits have already been identified with the help of the private sector and corporate houses. It has also been decided to take up four-five focus centres as 'Special Tourism Areas' in consultation with concerned state governments for integrated development.

Hotel accommodation is an important segment of the tourism industry, with huge potential for employment generation and foreign exchange earnings. To give impetus to this sector, the government provides tax benefits and other incentives to encourage the hotel industry. The industrial policy of the Centre has now placed the hotels and tourism-related activities as a priority industry. Foreign investment and collaboration are now facilitated under the new economic policy. Upto 51% foreign equity is now granted automatically. 100% investment from non-resident Indians is allowed. Now the Department of Tourism has streamlined and simplified the rules regarding the grant of approval to travel agents, tour operators and tourist transport operators so that their services to tourists are standardised and are more broad-based, for both international and domestic tourists. Approval, once granted, is valid forever, provided no complaints are received and the necessary documents are submitted annually. With a view to attract more chartered flights to India, a system of granting clearance has been formulated. An airconditioned rake of the *Palace on Wheels* train, which has been operational in Rajasthan for quite some time now has been very successful and popular. Similar trains are proposed to be operated in few other popular sectors.

A new range of hotels known as *Heritage hotels* has been introduced to add to the attraction of tourism in India. This class includes hotels opened in palaces, havelies, castles, forts and residences built prior to 1950. As these traditional places represent and reflect the Indian culture of the past, they have been very popular among the tourists. The heritage scheme rightly aims to ensure that such properties and landmarks of our culture and heritage are not lost due to decay and disuse. It also aims at providing additional room capacity for the tourists. So far, fifty properties have been classified in the heritage hotel category, providing a room capacity of over 1500 rooms. Guidelines have also been formulated for conversion of heritage properties into heritage hotels and their approval is at project-planning stage.

With a view to attract more foreign tourists, publicity is undertaken in major tourist generating markets of the world through various tourist offices located in North America, Europe, Australia, West and East Asia. The Department of Tourism of the Ministry of Tourism and Civil Aviation have both promotional and organisational functions. They work in close co-operation. There is a network of regional offices abroad and at home for publicity and marketing in the tourist generating markets. Overseas India has tourist offices in New York, Los Angeles, Chicago, Toronto, London, Geneva, Paris, Frankfurt, Brussels, Stockholm, Milan, Vienna, Kuwait, Bangkok, Tokyo, Singapore and Sydney. In addition, tourist promotion offices are based in Dallas, Miami, San Francisco, Washington, Osaka, Melbourne, Dubai and Kathmandu. To feed promotional material to these offices, Indian Embassies, Air India and the Department of Tourism produce tourist publicity literature in different languages. In order to cater to the domestic tourism, literature in Hindi is also produced. Tourist offices maintain film and photo libraries on subjects of tourist interest.

According to recent expert studies and research, the tourism industry is expected to give employment to 338 million people by the year 2005 throughout the world. It currently provides about 300 million jobs, which is more than one-tenth of all jobs worldwide. India seems to be well-poised to take good advantage of the coming boom in tourism and hotel industry but proper environment-protection measures should also be taken to prevent degradation of natural resources and wealth of the country. The experts have also underlined the need for greater awareness of the impact and implications of tourism with the globalisation and integration of this industry and economy. ●

20. JOB OPPORTUNITIES FOR WOMEN

MORE and more women in India are now taking up jobs and it is a right step in the direction for their economic emancipation and independence. This is also the direct result of emphasis on women's employment by our planners and many grassroots groups as the means of improving their economic and social position. Women are now entering the job market in bigger numbers to have equality with men. However, this goal may not be achieved simply by being gainfully employed because employed women are now doubly burdened as they have to work both in the office/factory and home. They enjoy neither greater choice nor better standards of living. It is really sad that their usual work at home before and after duty hours goes unrecognised and unrewarded. However, the advantages of gainful employment far outweigh these few disadvantages.

Employment of women is also desirable because their earnings and incomes go towards the welfare of children and family. Moreover, employment of women goes a long way in their empowerment.

The sex ratio in India is 933 females per 1000 males. This ratio has shown a continuous decline from 934 in 1981 to 933 at present. In spite of this adverse ratio of women, roughly half the world's and India's workforce consists of women. Only Kerala and Himachal Pradesh have more females than males. This huge work-force remains idle and unused to a large extent because of various reasons. Male dominance and arrogance, illiteracy, lack of education and training, unequal opportunities, and lack of awareness among women about their rights, privileges and potential are some of the main reasons for this sorry state of affairs. The status of working women in India is still considered lower than that of men. Economically, women are less privileged because they are not considered fit for gainful employment and economic activities. But in recent years the urban areas have seen an appreciable increase the number of women seeking employment as teachers, nurses, doctors, stenographers, clerks, sales girls, receptionists, telephone-operators, and secretaries, etc. Many of the professions, like those of executives, administrators, engineers, judges, and lawyers, etc., are dominated by males. Men hold the strings of their purses, and employed women have no freedom to spend their earnings as they like in most cases. This has given rise to considerable heartburn, tension and family disturbance.

The Constitution of India guarantees equal rights and opportunities for both men and women and efforts are being made through development and planning to raise the status of women, besides mainstreaming them into the process of national development on par with men. The programme for the development of women includes employment and income generation programmes, welfare and support services and programmes to create awareness, etc. The government of India and various state governments, with the intention to encourage more women to take up gainful employment outside their homes, have started many schemes. The policy of same wages for men and women for same job is being strictly adhered to. Under a scheme of rehabilitation, many centres have been set up with the aim of training destitute women in the age group of 18–50, in marketable skills. Some other programmes have also been implemented to provide employment to women through corporations, autonomous bodies and voluntary organisations. Under these schemes, training is imparted to women in selected non-traditional trades, such as electronics, watch-manufacturing, assembling, printing and binding, handlooms, weaving and spinning, and garment-making, etc.

Under condensed courses of education and vocational training, run by Central Social Welfare Board through voluntary organisations, women in the age group 18–30 years, who have some schooling, are coached for 2–3 hours to enable them to appear at different levels of examinations like middle school, secondary school and matriculation. The component of vocational training was added to this programme during 1975. During 1992–93, a provision of Rs. 8 crore was made for conducting 1,200 courses and schemes for providing a wide variety of income-generating activities to needy women, particularly the poor and the downtrodden, widows, destitutes, and disabled, etc. Small industrial units, handlooms and handicraft units, dairy units and other small, animal husbandry programmes, like piggery, goat and sheep breeding, poultry units and self-employment units have also been set up. A new thrust has been given to identifying new sectors of income generating projects. The programme of support to training-cum-employment for women living below the poverty line was launched in 1987, to strengthen and improve the skills and employment opportunities in traditional sectors where majority of women are already working daily. The focus has been mainly on marginalised and assetless women from households of daily wage labourers, unpaid female workers, female-headed households and other dispossessed groups, in order to integrate them into the mainstream of development.

In order to provide cheap, safe and suitable accommodation to working women from low-income groups, hostels have been opened in co-operation with voluntary organisations. Separate hostels for working women with children up to 8 years have also been opened. But the need for such support services like child-care centres, and hostels, etc., is not adequately met. More and more schemes should be implemented on a priority basis so that women can contribute more effectively to the national wealth and productivity. New schemes should be undertaken to rehabilitate the poor and destitute women and their dependent children through vocational training and residential care. The National Commission for Women was set up in January, 1992 to monitor the matters relating to legal and Constitutional safeguards provided for women, to monitor the implementation of legislation made to protect the rights for women, to review the existing legislation concerning women and suggest amendments wherever recured and to look into the complaints and take *suo-moto* notice of cases involving deprivation of the rights of women. Government has also introduced special legislations for protection of the interests of women. These include Equal Remuneration Act, Maternity Benefit Act, Immoral Traffic Prevention Act, and Dowry Prohibition Act. There are many polytechnics and industrial training institutes exclusively for women. But these are hardly sufficient to meet the increasing number of women seeking training facilities in various trades and vocational courses. The need for increased number of such institutions for women is further underlined by the fact that there is rising unemployment among educated women and a great rush for white-collar jobs. To solve this problem of unemployment in educated women, they should be encouraged to start their factories, workshops and enterprises. By giving liberal loans from banks and financial institutions, their self-employment opportunities can be further increased. For securing greater self-employment opportunities for women, they can be given preference in matters of granting licences for industries and allotment of basic raw materials for small scale industries. Career development of women has now become an important matter as more and more women are joining the workforce. Initially they settled for professions like medicine, office jobs, and teaching, etc., but now they have entered sectors that are dominated by males at top and senior levels. According to the President of Women's Forum, "Women are no longer satisfied with traditional stereotyped roles, and want to move up in the corporate hierarchy. The aptitude, intelligence, education and skills of women have not been used and this is a great economic waste for the nation. Even from the monetary point of view, the female labour force constitutes an important reservoir of talent which is necessary for companies to use to remain competitive in the business world."

Today, there is greater career awareness among women and they want to march ahead, both in managing careers and families. With proper planning and implementation, the huge workforce of women can be suitably utilised in various sectors of management, entrepreneurship, industries, administration, and services for India's better progress and development. There are many employment opportunities and services yet to be explored and exploited for women. For example, women's participation in our defence services, as in medical services, is long overdue. Indian women can as effectively contribute towards our national security, productivity and development as men. ●

21. LEISURE TIME

Work and leisure are interrelated. They are like the two sides of the same coin. The observation that "we must beat the iron when it is hot, but we may polish it at leisure", best explains the proper relation between work and leisure. Leisure is like a margin on a printed or written page. In the absence of work no leisure can be actually conceived. Leisure never means idleness. Leisure cannot be thought of as a non-activity. It should be seen in a broader perspective, as a fulfilling part of life and work. As J.B. Priestley has said, "Any fool can be fussy and rid himself of energy all over the place, but a man has to have something in him before he can settle down to do nothing. He must have reserves to draw upon must be able to plunge into the strange, slow river of dreams and reverie, must be at heart a poet." Only a very few have these reserves to draw upon. Moreover, dreaming, thinking and even meditation are activities, though of different kind. One works hard only to have some leisure because "man does not live by bread alone." So leisure may be called the spare time, free from labour and drudgery of life. It is a kind of diversion. The dictionary definition of leisure is, "the state of having time at one's disposal; time which one can spend as one pleases; free or unoccupied time". A famous French scholar and sociologist has defined leisure as "an activity apart from the obligations of work, family and society, to which the individual turns at will, for either relaxation, diversion or broadening of knowledge and his spontaneous social participation, the free expression of his creative capacity." Leisure is a kind of breathing space or a welcome and desirable pause in the long hours of work and labour. A labour is sweet and honourable when it is earned with the sweat of the brow.

The rapid and radical scientific and technological advancements have made life easy and convenient. Our life is now far more free and leisurely than it was for our forefathers. Affluence and ease have brought more leisure hours. We are relieved of much of drudgery now and have more spare hours to relieve us of fatigue. The housewife too, now has more free time as there are many labour-saving devices at her disposal. Consequently, all of us can now enjoy long hours of rest, relaxation, joy, diversion and entertainment. All work and no play would certainly make Jack a dull boy. Leisure is a kind of insurance against dullness, fatigue, boredom, tension and cares of life. After hours of work and struggle, we need some rest, relaxation, joy, respite, freshness and a kind of brief holiday. Leisure helps us in keeping our body and mind toned up, healthy and refreshed. Some time devoted to regular diversions, or hobbies, is bound to strengthen and refresh us in more than one way for better achievements in our respective fields of life. The five-day a week work culture gives us a lot of spare time to spend in recreation, rest, hobbies, simple and innocent joys of life and intellectual and artistic activities.

But for many, leisure may be a problem as they may not know how to use and enjoy their spare time. For them leisure may be more boring and monotonous than the daily routine occupation. Leisure is like a double-edged sword which can be either used well or misused. A person can be best judged by the way he or she uses the leisure hours. It never means frittering away the precious time in drinking, gambling or idle gossiping. It should be viewed as a golden opportunity and used for healthy enjoyment, intellectual, spiritual, cultural and artistic pursuits. One may spend this time in playing with children, listening to their stories or in observing nature and birds.

An idle mind is the devil's workshop. The right use of leisure hours can help us in shaping and developing our personality in the desired way. It is really condemnable to spend leisure without a definite plan to have purposeful gains. Leisure provides us a rare opportunity to satisfy our inner demands. By means of our regular occupations and professions, we satisfy our physical and material demands. Now, during leisure we can very well satisfy our artistic, cultural, aesthetic, intellectual and spiritual urges. We can devote our spare hours to reading, writing, playing a musical instrument or in the pursuit of some meaningful creative and socially relevant activity. There are many hobbies to choose from. We may select from these according to our aptitude and resources, etc. Once we have made a judicious selection, we can make our leisure really interesting, meaningful and worthwhile. All cultural and aesthetical achievements and improvements arise from leisure. It helps people in becoming whole, integrated and cultured. During these precious moments of respite, relaxation, rest and diversion, one can stand and stare at things beautiful, ponder on the meaning of life and turn one's life into a real asset.

Different people spend leisure differently. Some may occupy themselves in gardening, photography, reading or playing outdoor or indoor games. Others may busy themselves in playing with children or in enjoying music.

In modern times, viewing television is becoming more and more popular. In western countries people spend roughly 45% of their leisure hours in front of their T.V. sets. In India also more and more people spend their time before their T.V. sets, viewing films, popular serials or other programmes. Women and children too are enthusiastic viewers of television programmes in India. But watching T.V. for long hours has its inherent risks as it is a passive entertainment and there is no participation by the viewers in it.

Short work weeks and automation of activities have resulted in more leisure and spare time. And with this, the danger of mental dissipation, flirtation and killing of time in idle entertainment have increased. Success and purposefulness of leisure is as important as that of our employment or vocational pursuits. Leisure can be a means of both our elevation, enrichment, improvement of sensibilities and degradation, fall, moral dissipation and flirtation. Leisure in itself is neither good nor bad. It is its use that makes it good or bad. No doubt all intellectual improvement arises from leisure but too much and too frequent leisure makes a poet cry :

Leisure is pain; takes off our chariot wheels,
How heavily we drag the load of life
Blest leisure is our curse like that of Cain,
It makes us wander, wander earth around
To fly that tyrant thought.

Therefore, leisure with purpose and meaningfulness should be our aim for has not Cicero, the famous Roman statesman said, "The thing which is the most outstanding and chiefly to be desired by all healthy and good and well-off persons is leisure with honour." If we stick to the principle of "leisure with honour" then it would be no problem at all. We must be alert and watchful against the abuse of leisure. ●

22. INDIAN CINEMA

CINEMA is now over a hundred years old. History of Indian cinema began with the production of *Pundalik* in 1912 by R.G. Torney and N.G. Chitre. This was followed by *Raja Harish Chandra* produced in 1913 by D.G. Phalke, the father of Indian cinema. In the beginning, films were silent as there was no sound, no dialogue. But in 1931, with the production of *Alam Ara,* began the era of talkie films. Indian cinema has seen a phenomenal growth and advancement during these years. The Indian film industry is the biggest in the world, employing thousands of workers, technicians, actors, singers, dancers, producers, dialogue and script writers, musicians and other artists. A huge and staggering amount of money has been invested in the industry. India is the largest producer of feature films in the world. The number of feature films produced annually in India may soon touch four figures or more. Hindi feature films dominate the scene, followed by those in Telugu, Tamil and other languages. Mumbai, Chennai and Kolkata are the leading film-producing centres.

Cinema has been very popular in the country. Its mass appeal is irresistable. Due to its audio-visual character, it has been a great and abiding influence on the people. They are influenced to a great extent in their way of living by what they see in films on the large silver screen and on the television. The video and cable boom, coupled with satellite communication, has further fired the craze. The popularity of, and craze for, films has given rise to video piracy and the people engaged in it are virtually minting money. Besides feature films, telefilms and serials are viewed by a large spectrum of audience, spread over all the sections of the society. Foreign films dubbed in Hindi and other Indian languages are also becoming popular.

Cinema is an important and integral part of electronic mass media in India. It is very powerful as a means of mass communication, entertainment, education, information and formation of public opinion. Its visual and persuasive appeal is unmatched and it wields considerable power to influence its vast audience. Its potentialities and possibilities are vast, to touch the masses as an expression of art, culture, human thoughts and sensibilities. Under its stimulus mass public awakening can be generated, national integrity, unity, communal harmony and eradication of such evils as dowry and superstitions, etc., can be achieved. There cannot be a more powerful, touching and appealing medium than cinema.

Indian cinema has produced many outstanding and trail-blazing films, both in Hindi and regional languages. But their number is not heartening at all. The majority of our films conform to an established formula, and are produced to make quick and large profits. A host of the films of the seventies, led by *Sholay*, belong to this category. They are full of sex, songs, and violence — super block-busters, produced keeping mainly the box office in view. Formula films full of stock, stereotype situations, scenes bordering obscenity, melodrama, exciting music and dances are there in thousands. They do not offer any inspiring, regenerating healthy entertainment to the audience as they fail to reflect our profound social changes and values, rich cultural heritage full of variety, colour and fascination. They fail to mirror the ultimate synthesis emerging out of the conflict between tradition and modernism, beliefs and scientific temper. Against this grey and dull background, such films as *Pather Panchali*, *Pyasa*, *Mother India*, *Jagriti*, *Jagte Raho*, *Mera Naam Joker*, *Akrosh*, *Ardha Satya*, *Lagaan* and a host of others, shine like jewels. The new wave art cinema also known as budget films, which are seen as a reaction to the run-of-the will and romantic stuff, gave us some very fine films. The National Film Development Corporation (NFDC), established in April 1980, helps in producing low-budget, yet good quality films. The NFDC also encourages foreign coproductions. *Gandhi* and *Salaam Bombay* are the two examples of very successful coproductions. NFDC helps production of films based on good scripts to be produced and directed by well-known producers and directors. The Corporation's conscientious attempt to expose Indian audiences to a variety of high quality foreign films is also laudable. It sends its delegates to international film festivals to promote Indian Cinema. It also plays host to many buyers of films from foreign countries. Indian films are exported to over 100 countries.

We have the Central Board of Film Certification, consisting of eminent personalities in the field. The Board examines films for certification before they are publicly screened and exhibited. But, unfortunately, there are hundreds of films which should not have been certified at all for public exhibition. These films invariably revolve round the 'boy meets girl' formula, with cheap songs, dances, stereotyped love triangle and a lot of sex and violence. They have neither social relevance nor appeal to the aesthetic sensibilities of the audience. There is a lot of repetition in them. The same age-old story is often served with different titles. Far removed from real situations of life, they cater to the tastes of uneducated, ill-cultured and unrefined cine-goers. Outrage, crime, violence, sex, rape, excitement, crude cabaret dances, unrealistic situations and scenes are common features of these *masala* and formula films.

These have adversely affected the conduct, character and morals of the public in general, and those of children and young men and women of the country in particular. Many of our modern crimes have a direct relation to these films. These films have helped a great deal in the rise of the crime-graph.

The suspected nexus between the film world and the underworld dons, mafia groups, smugglers and drug-traffickers is very disturbing. The bane of the Indian film industry is that it is ultimately in the hands of some very rich and unscrupulous sections of society. They always have the box-office before their eyes and want to earn huge, quick and easy profits. They believe in hit box-office films and throw away all their social obligations to the wind. Their main emphasis is on entertainment, and that too cheap and vulgar entertainment. The production of films on purely commercial lines has created a vicious circle.

It is the duty of film-makers not only to cater to the tastes of the masses but also to create healthy and desirable cinema. No doubt the overwhelming majority of cine-goers and film-viewers lack refined, sharp sensibilities, aesthetic sense and good moral taste, but it is the fault of the industry that it should succumb so abjectly to such pressure, throwing overboard all norms of social behaviour, decency, human and cultural values and demands of accepted modesty. What we need today are decent, clean, cultural, social, bold, innovative, well-balanced, artistic and technically beautiful films based on scripts of reputed and socially responsible writers. The expenses of film production can be reduced by reducing the length and duration of films. Methods and ways and means should be devised to effect economy in the production of films, so that one does not have to go to unscrupulous and unprincipled financial barons. It is sheer madness to run after mega-budget, block-buster film production. Modesty, balance, social relevance, human values, realism blended with idealism, rationality, and sobriety, etc., should be our guiding principles in the production of films. As far as children's films are concerned, we are a very poor nation. For the production of good healthy and successful films for children, we need devoted, patient, imaginative, contented yet reasonably ambitious, poetical people with a touch of child-like simplicity and innocence. It seems that in spite of such great popularity and boom, Indian cinema is standing at the crossroads without any sense of destination and direction, sans sanity, sans sublimity. Yet there are hopes and expectations because we have lot of exceptional talent, resources and skills required for the job, only the orientation is lacking. ●

23. CORRUPTION UNLIMITED

CORRUPTION is ubiquitous and unlimited. It has become all-pervading, a world phenomenon. It has increased by leaps and bounds worldwide, in direct relation and proportion to our moral degradation, destruction of character, devaluation of human values and lust for power and money. It is said that when character is lost everything is lost. There is no character and so we have lost all. The political leaders, the heads of governments and others at helm of the affairs of many nations are corrupt and corruption is contagious. It spreads rapidly and percolates to all the lower levels. It is there in Japan, Italy, Pakistan, Mexico, China, Iran, Iraq, America, and England, etc. There is no country immune from it. There might be a difference of degrees, but as far as its quality, gravity and pervasiveness are concerned, there is hardly any difference.

Corruption in India is rampant and well established in all spheres of our life — public life, politics, administration, business, judicial system, education, research and security. There is hardly any exception. There are scandals and scams in plenty, right from the Bofors scandal to the recent Taj heritage corridor scandal. In foreign countries, when corruption charges are proved there is suitable punishment, but in India there is no system, no tradition to bring the corrupt to trial and then to make him pay for his crime. There is crime but no punishment. It is a salient feature of Indian corruption.

In a write-up, Mr. K. Subrahmanyan has wittily remarked, "Long before our economic globalisation began, India was globalised in respect of political corruption and politician-organised crime nexus. Therefore, smugglers, narcotics' barons, vice syndicates and protection rackets have become patrons of political parties. The former provides large resources to politicians and the latter ensures no legal enforcement against organised crime." For example, take the Securities scam. Harshad Mehta manipulated things in such a way as to enable himself to siphon crores of rupees fraudulantly from banks, under the very noses of the managers, high officials and other members of the staff of the Reserve Bank of India. Was it because of alleged system failure or because there was a collusion between him and the officials concerned? The connivance of one or two cabinet ministers has also been there. Fingers were also raised at M.J. Pherwani, the then Chairman of the National Housing Bank, who died under mysterious circumstances soon after. Consequently, a Joint Parliamentary Committee (JPC) was constituted under the chairmanship of Mr. R.N. Mirdha to probe the scandal. The JPC finally submitted its report to the Parliament but nothing happened to the people found involved in the scam. When there was a hue and cry from the Opposition, a couple of ministers were asked to submit their resignations and that was all. As has already been pointed out, we have no system, no tradition, either to punish the guilty or to bring an investigation to its logical conclusion. Moreover, public memory is very short.

There is a parallel economy in operation in India and black money is ever on the increase because of political patronage and collusion. There is a widespread evasion of taxes, to the tune of crores of rupees every year, owing to corruption in politics, administration and enforcement agencies. In return, the political gurus get huge funds to fight elections and bribes for personal accumulations. This helps them to keep themselves in positions of power and influence. The funding from organised black marketeers, drug traffickers, underworld dons, mafias and smugglers is actually on a much larger scale than is apparent. This has crippled our economy and turned our planning haywire.

Corruption has become a way of life. There is no effective check on this growing menace because there is lack of political will. In spite of anti-corruption departments and squads, it has permeated the rank and the file of the administration. No work can be got done unless the palms of the concerned officials are greased. Lubricant in the form of gratification is a must to make the administrative machinery move smoothly in your favour. First satisfy the officials and then get satisfying results in return. Often, investigations by CBI and vigilance departments into corruption charges against the bureaucrats have proved futile. Such is the power of manipulation, money and nepotism. Kickbacks, gratifications, bribes, and commissions are the order of the day. Students pay capitation fees to get admission in professional courses, job-seekers purchase positions in the administration, contractors grease the palms of the engineers so as to enable themselves to use sand in place of cement in contractual constructions, businessmen use the appropriate 'lubricant' to keep their illegal operations moving smoothly. And then these people, in turn, want to regain their money manifold and quickly by resorting to fradulent, easy and corrupt means. Thus, there is a vicious circle engulfing all and sundry.

Honest, sincere and god-fearing officials are looked down upon. They are considered simpletons, while the bribe-takers are the heroes. The corrupt officials are doing very well for themselves and their higher-ups patronise and protect them because of their fair share in the bribes. These people, in collaboration, co-operation and collusion with others, are enriching themselves. They have fat bank balances, houses in prime locations, and all the modern amenities. They are really rolling in wealth and comprise the most successful segment of the society. There are a few honest ones but they are not courageous enough to condemn and criticise their dishonest and bribe-happy colleagues. They are silent spectators to their corrupt counterparts, being favoured with important posts and assignments. The honest officers are a demoralised lot. Consequently, the fence-sitters are being pushed on to the bandwagon of the corrupt lot.

Corruption cannot be checked and minimised unless political leaders themselves are honest and have a strong will and desire to stem the rot. The leaders should encourage honest officials and help them to unite against corrupt and dishonest ones. Corruption should be dealt with an iron hand and further rules and regulations enacted to punish the corrupt government servants and administrators. Nepotism, favouritism, and red-tapism, etc., should be eliminated because they form the very foundations of corruption. Improvement in salaries, creation of more employment opportunities can also go a long way in tackling the menace successfully.

Honesty is conspicuous these days by its absence. According to a newspaper report, even the judiciary does not seem to be free from the evil. The former Chief Justice of the Supreme Court, E.S. Venkatramaiya speaking in an interview said, "The judiciary in India has deteriorated in its standard because such judges are appointed as are willing to be influenced by lavish parties and whiskey bottles." He added, "In every high court, there are at least four to five judges who are practically out every evening, wining and dining either at a lawyer's house or a foreign embassy." Corruption is now so well-organised and entrenched in the system that it requires a will of steel and the courage of a lion to fight it. Now, effective and strong strategies, backed by strong political will, should be devised to checkmate it. There should be deterrent punishment for those indulging in corruption. Both giving and taking of bribes should be a cognisable offence. Much depends upon our political leaders, bureaucrats and the enlightened public consciousness. Unless these three units make sincere efforts and show their commitment to the democratic nation and society, nothing much will be achieved to check and eliminate corruption. ●

24. SECULARISM IN INDIA

INDIA is unique in being a secular nation. It is a sovereign, socialist, secular, democratic, republic. The Indian Constitution guarantees its citizens full freedom in matters of religious faith. One of the fundamental rights and freedom granted to all citizens, individually and collectively, is the "right to freedom of conscience and free profession, practice and propagation of religion." Moreover, every section of the society has the "right to conserve its culture, language or script and right to establish and administer educational institutions of their choice." This freedom of culture, conscience and faith is one of the basic cornerstones of Indian democracy. But there is much confusion and misunderstanding about the secular character of India. Sometimes it may be construed that India is anti-religious, irreligious or indifferent to religion. However, Indian secularism is totally different in its meaning and content. It only means that there is no state religion. There is no favour to any particular religion and its followers. All religions and their followers are equal in the eyes of law. There is neither favour nor hostility towards any faith. It only means that the state is neutral in the matter of religious faith and its propagation. There cannot be any discrimination on the basis of religion, faith, caste, creed, race, sex, community, and language, etc. There is complete religious freedom unless it interferes in the freedom of other religions. Here in India, religion and its practice has been recognised as a personal and private affair. But it never means public and collective religious functions, etc., cannot be held. It only means that there is no state patronage or opposition to any particular religion.

India is a vast country, with more than a billion people of various faiths, religious sects and cultures, etc. Its staggering diversity has been a mighty unifying factor to make it a strong and unified nation. There are various races, castes communities and religions co-existing in peace and harmony for many centuries. There are Hindus, Muslims, Sikhs, Jains, Parsis, Christians, Buddhists, Jews and a host of others. Hindus are in majority, forming over 82% of the total population. The Muslims are the single largest minority and constitute over 11% of the total population. Next come the Christians and the Sikhs. The communal intolerance and fight between the Hindus and the Muslims has been a legacy of the Britishers. They followed the policy of divide and rule and this ultimately led to the partition of the sub-continent into India and Pakistan at the time of Independence in 1947. Millions of Muslims left India for good and migrated to the newly formed Pakistan and yet millions of them stayed back in India, being assured of their security, safety and religious freedom. In post-independent India, the Hindu-Muslim conflict has been more or less backed and sponsored by certain vested interests. Hindus and Muslims, by and large, are tolerant and co-operative and like to co-exist in peace, harmony and respect for each other.

Secularism is the very essence of Indian democracy. It reflects the ancient Indian tradition of religious tolerance, co-operation and mutual respect for one another. Islam came to India with the Muslim conquests. The Muslims in India make it one of the largest Islamic nations. The contribution of Islam towards India's culture and civilisation has been very significant and lasting. It has added colour, variety, strength and richness to Indian heritage and culture. The Christian Church here is much older than Islam. St. Thomas, one of the twelve disciples of Christ, was the first preacher of Christianity in India. He was a contemporary of St. Peter in Rome. The Parsis came in the eighth century, seeking refuge from religious persecution in Iran and brought Zorastrianism. The Jews came quite early, about 2,000 years ago and settled down chiefly in Mumbai, Pune, Kochi and Delhi. In Hinduism itself, there are hundreds of sects following different religious practices, rites, rituals, and manners of worship and prayer. Sometimes the difference between one sect from the other may be as wide as that between one religion and the other. This religious diversity represents a complete and wonderful pattern of unity, integrity and wholeness.

India has been always secular and yet profoundly religious. It is in keeping with this eternal spirit that our Constitutional fathers declared India a secular state, without any discrimination on the basis of faith and religion among other things. It was a great Indian value upheld by these leaders of great wisdom in the larger interest of India and its teeming millions. The secular character of Indian polity was further strengthened under the great leadership of Mahatma Gandhi during the struggle for independence. Himself a deeply religious Hindu, he had a great respect for all other religions and faiths. Ultimately, he died at the altar of British imperialism, based on religious divide and intolerance and for the cause of religious tolerance, communal harmony, which form the very foundation of true secularism.

There have been communal and religious riots, conflicts and conflagrations during the last 50 years of our independence but mainly because of certain vested political and sectarian interests. These politicians and their parties have been using different communities as their vote banks. Lack of education, enlightenment, economical advancement, scientific temper, and existence of orthodoxy and obscurantism, aided and abetted by certain fanatic, fundamentalist and narrow-minded elements have been the main causes of communal disharmony in India. A majority of Muslims are still backward, illiterate, superstitious and unaware of modern, economic, scientific and technological advances. They are being exploited by some religious fanatics and so-called political leaders to grind their own axe. Among the Hindus also there are sections of people subject to such exploitation. They become easy tools in the hands of these bigots and indulge in communal conflicts.

There is an urgent need to be aware of these anti-social and anti-secular forces so that they may be exposed and effectively checkmated. The economic and cultural backwardness of these sections should be removed. They should be brought into the national mainstream so as to eliminate their self-imposed isolation, alienation and backwardness. It is natural that these economically weak and vulnerable sections should succumb to narrow sectarian pressures and rise in revolt in the name of religion against those who are better off and belong to the other community and faith. Removal of unemployment and backwardness, more equal distribution of national wealth and removal of imbalances in economic development of various communities only can ensure real and lasting secularism. It cannot prosper in poverty, economic discrimination, backwardness and slums because then the communities or people suffering from these evils can easily become prey to fundamentalist and reactionary communal forces in the country. We should not allow these communal forces to undermine our secular spirit, religious tolerance, peace, harmony, co-existence and respect for each other. No political leader or party should be allowed to raise the bogey of religion or community. Religion is a personal affair and has nothing to do with the day-to-day national affairs. In our public and social life, we should be guided only by national interests. Nation should always come first. All religions teach tolerance, peace, harmony, co-operation and respect for other religions and faiths. No truely religious person will ever indulge in communal violence, hatred or rioting.

Communal riots and clashes are a big hindrance in national integration, unity and economic development. Many a time, communal riots break out because of slackness on the part of the administration, police and law-enforcement agencies. Special task forces, committees, societies, and clubs, etc., should be established to face this menace. More and more people of different communities should be involved in the work of promoting religious harmony and secularism. The agents of fanaticism, narrow, vested, political and communal interests should be dealt with sternly. Communal disturbances and riots in India are aberrations, in which the weak and the poor suffer most. They should be checked, minimised and rooted out at the earliest. Communal flare-ups and riots are not always between the Hindus and the Muslims, but sometimes they are also between Sunnis and Shia groups or two different groups belonging to the Hindu community. But they all have their roots in ignorance, obscurantism and lack of proper understanding of their respective religions and their tenets and teachings. The virus of communalism should be weeded out by all means because it is a great obstacle in the way of secularisation of our polity, on which ultimately our unity, integrity, solidarity and progress ultimately depends. ●

25. THE ROLE OF NEWSPAPERS

THE newspapers, as the voice of the people, play a very important role in a democracy like India. They form an important link between the public and the government. It is through newspapers that the public comes to know about the priorities, policies and programmes of the government. Similarly, the government can keep itself well informed about grievances, aspirations, expectations, and opinions, etc., of the public through the press. Newspapers also supply news, views, and comments, etc., to its readers about national, international and local affairs. They help in formation of public opinion on matters of national and global importance. They not only mould but also reflect public opinion. The editorial and leading articles play a significant role in the matter. Then there are interviews of people and personalities who actually matter. Newspapers are the real watchdogs of a democracy

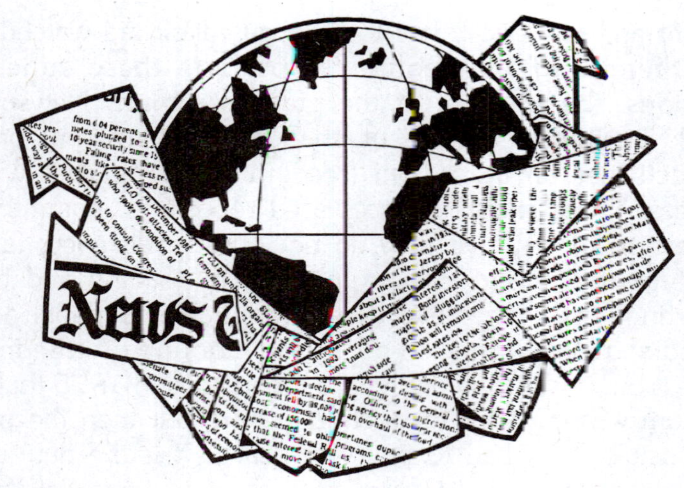

and of the rights and privileges of the people. Newspapers can also be instrumental in bringing out desired social, cultural and attitudinal changes in society. They may be effectively used as an instrument of national integrity, unity, harmony and solidarity and also in removing social evils, such as superstitions, evils of untouchability, dowry, communalism and casteism.

The powers and influence of the press are really unlimited. But they can be misused as well. They are like double-edged swords. In wrong hands, they may be used by vested interests and anti-social elements to further their own selfish ends at the cost of national and social interests. They may give distorted views and half-baked or false news. If confined in the hands of capitalists, they may be used to suppress and crush labour movements and anti-poverty campaigns as these pose a threat to their monopolistic ventures and business interests. In dictatorships, the press is not free and the newspapers are used only to promote the interests of a few, forming the nucleus around the dictator. Then they are not the voice of the people but the mouthpiece of the despotic ruler. It is only in a democracy that a newspaper is a common man's representative, voice and counsellor, all rolled into one.

As a friend, guide, counsellor, educator, representative and voice of the people, a newspaper has to be impartial, truthful, sincere and fearless. It has to be a guardian and watchdog of the interests of the people. To perform these duties and functions, the freedom of the press is a must. Newspapers should be free to criticise or encourage government policies and activities on merit. But freedom is meaningless without fairness. There should be no biased reportings, comments or expression of views. If they do not observe decency, fairness and impartiality and indulge in false, misleading and biased reporting, they can make themselves liable to penal action. In India, newspapers enjoy a fair amount of freedom of expression. It was only during the Emergency in 1975 that their freedom was curtailed for a short period, but then the people responsible for it had to pay very dearly. It is the duty of the editors, reporters and journalists to be fair, impartial, honest and constructive in their profession. It is only the yellow journalism that indulges in blackmail, extortion of money and concessions or such other benefits. A journalist, loyal to his profession, will not colour his reporting or exaggerate and distort his news. He will not betray the readers for personal gains, gifts and advantages. Yellow journalism is as great a danger to a nation and society as are the acts of smugglers, mafias, drug-traffickers and people engaged in espionage against their own country. A journalist should never forget his mission of unbiased, frank, fearless and truthful reporting. An honest, fearless and frank newspaper is a perfect antidote for political corruption, irregularities, favouritism, nepotism, and blackmail, etc., indulged in by the people in authority and power. The government and the people that run it cannot remain indifferent to criticism, comments and opinion expressed against them in the newspapers in a democracy. Sometimes the administration may try to tame a newspaper by threatening to stop advertisements to it because they are a must for the survival of a newspaper. But no newspaper, truly loyal to its commitment to the people and society, should succumb to such pressures. Rather, it should expose such conspiracy to suppress the freedom of the press.

Obviously, newspapers can play a vital role in the reconstruction and regeneration of a country. During our struggle for independence, the press played its important, constructive role. It reminds us of Tilak, Gandhi, Nehru and other leaders who published and edited newspapers and magazines or wrote articles, and reviews, etc., for them. These played a very positive role in quickening the process of national struggle for freedom. Their heroic, bold and missionary writings had the desired impact on the masses and, consequently, they got actively involved in the movement. Tilak was jailed and sent to Mandalay, in Burma (Myanmar), for his writings that were full of patriotic fervour and nationalism, but for the Britishers these were seditious. Similarly, Gandhiji and many other national leaders had to pay for their journalistic freedom, courage and honesty.

The history of Indian newspapers and journalism is quite old. *Bengal Gazette* was the first newspaper published in India in the middle of the 18th century. Raja Ram Mohan Roy published his newspaper *Kaumudi,* and Ishwar Chandra Vidyasagar *Prabhakar*. Indian newspapers include 41 centenarians. The Gujarati daily *Bombay Samachar* published from Mumbai is the oldest existing newspaper. It began its publication in 1822. *Anand Bazar Patrika*, *Punjab Kesari* and the *Times of India* are the three biggest newspapers as far as circulation is concerned. By the end of the year 2000, there were as many as 49,145 newspapers, including dailies, tri/bi-weeklies, weeklies and other periodicals. Uttar Pradesh ranks the first, with 8,415 newspapers, including 844 dailies. The highest number of newspapers are published in Hindi followed by English, Urdu and Bengali. The circulation numbers of newspapers are gradually increasing appreciably with the spread of literacy and political and social awakening amidst the public. The number of newspapers owned and published by individuals is the largest. Their share in circulation is estimated at over 40%. This reflects the monopolistic position of certain individuals and business houses in the world of newspapers in India. Therefore, these people have certain advantages, but Indian journalism is now quite mature, responsible and free, which ensures that no group or business house can take liberty in the matter. Then there is the Press Council of India, established for the purpose of preserving the freedom of the press, maintaining and improving the standards and quality of newspapers, news agencies and journalism in the country. The Council is a quasi-judicial body and does not possess any punitive powers. However, it exercises a moral authority. It considers and decides complaints and grievances received both from the public against the newspaper and from the press. It may also direct an erring newspaper to publish the complainant's reply/rejoinder, with an apology in appropriate cases. On the one hand it helps newspapers and news agencies to maintain their independence, on the other, it ensures, the maintenance of high standards of public taste and fostering a sense of rights and responsibilities of citizenship. So it is freedom with responsibility. ●

26. FOREST CONSERVATION

THE birth and growth of human civilisation and culture has been very intimately connected with the forests. Forests have had a great influence on human thought and way of living. For example, the *Vedas* and *Upanishads*, the oldest known religious, philosophical and literary monuments of mankind are the direct products of forest-life in ancient India. The *Aranyakas* or the Forest Texts form an integral part of these oldest testaments of human wisdom and philosophy. They are called so because they were both composed and studied in the forest-dwellings. They contain the contemplation and meditation of the forest seers, hermits and rishis on God and Soul.

Many of the Vedic gods are deified forces of nature They have been very beautifully and poetically personified in hymns and prayers. The Vedic mind looked upon forests as the 'ecological redresser of man's excessive activism' and as 'an intimate part of his life and experience'. In a very fascinating hymn, which is addressed to the Spirit of the forest, the Vedic poet says :

"The Spirit of the forest never slays unless one approaches in fury, One may eat at will of her luscious fruits and rest in her shade at one's pleasure.

Adorned with fragrant perfumes and she needs not toil for her food. Mother of untamed forest beasts, Spirit of the wood, I salute you !"

The intimacy with forests has always been a refreshing and invigorating influence in human life. But modern materialism, greed and over-exploitation of forests have left the bitter taste of the fruits of prosperity. It has created a disharmony and imbalance in our ecology and environment, an evil that is being intensely realised now. The urbanisation and industrialisation on a vast scale, during the past few decades, have resulted in mass deforestation and depletion of the green cover. Forests are one of the priceless boons of nature, but human consumerism has created such a great pressure on forests that they have almost disappeared in many areas, resulting in soil-erosion, floods, barrenness of the earth, pollution, climatic changes, droughts and destruction of the fragile ecosystem.

The neglect and destruction of forests is bound to have serious repercussions on our lives.

There is an urgent need to check deforestation and dwindling of green-cover in India. Gandhiji once said that, "Nature has enough for everybody's needs but not for everybody's greed." The over exploitation of our forests has put us in an alarming situation. Hence, the preservation and development of forests should rank high in our priorities.

The part played by forests in improving the quality of environment and that of life is beyond any shadow of doubt. They are a great source of renewable energy and contribute significantly to our economic development. India has an area of 752.3 lakh hectare notified as forests, of which 406.1 lakh hectare is classified as reserved and 215.1 lakh hectare as protected. Unclassified area is spread over 131.1 lakh hectare. About 19.47% of the total geographical area of the country is under actual forest-cover. But, unfortunately, this cover is fast shrinking because of our greed, selfishness and wrong priorities. Consequently, the wildlife has also been threatened and many species of animals and birds have become extinct and many others are in danger of extinction.

India has a forest policy since 1894. It was revised in 1952 and again in 1988. The policy aims at protection, conservation and development of forests. Its main objectives are—(i) Maintenance of environmental stability through preservation and restoration of ecological balance; (ii) Conservation of natural heritage (iii) Check on soil erosion and denudation in catchment areas of rivers, lakes and reservoirs; (iv) Check on extension of sand dunes in the desert area of Rajasthan and along coastal tracts; (v) Substantial increase in forest tree cover through massive afforestation and social forestry programmes (vi) Steps to meet requirements of fuel, wood, fodder, minor forest produce and timber for rural and tribal populations; (vii) Increase in productivity of forest to meet the national needs; (viii) Encouragement of efficient utilisation of forest produce and optimum substitution of wood, and (ix) Steps to create a massive people's movement, with involvement of women to achieve these objectives and minimise pressure on existing forests.

In the light of this policy, the forest related activities are being given a new orientation. These activities include development of waste lands, reforestation and replantation, forest settlement, restriction on grazing and supply of other kinds of fuel, elimination of forest contractors, and discouragement of monoculture practice, etc.

The objectives are really laudable but there is no proper and strict implementation of the policy decisions. Destruction of forests by timber merchants, contractors, and local people, etc., is still going on. Trees are being cut indiscriminately in the Himalayas, causing floods, soil erosion and siltation of the rivers and canals of the area. Some enlightened people of the area were very much concerned at these activities of deforestation and so started the Chipko Movement under the leadership of Sundarlal Bahuguna. The movement demands that forests be conserved and protected and degradation of the environment be stopped immediately. Among other things, the movement wants to ban felling of trees and encroachment on forest land, identification of forests to be declared as reserved and grant of rights and concessions to the tribles and forest-people with proper control mechanisms. Ban on felling of trees for a number of years is a must to allow these forests in the Himalayas to recover. These hills and catchment areas prone to landslide, flood and erosion should be totally protected and quickly afforested. Gradually, the local population is becoming more and more aware of the importance of forests and the green-cover and the necessity of their conservation. But in the face of manipulation and collusion between the contractors and forest officials, they find themselves helpless.

Fire is another major factor in the destruction of forests. Most of the forest-fires are man-made, deliberate and started by vested interests. It is rarely accidental. In order to stop forest-fires, there should be more watch-towers and the number of fire-watchers should be increased substantially. In 1984, two

Fire Control Projects were established in Chandarpura (Maharashtra) and Haldwani, Nainital (Uttar Pradesh), but this scheme should be extended immediately to other forest areas prone to fire.

Private corporate sector should also be effectively involved in the afforestation and conservation of forests. The involvement of non-government organisations can go a long way in the conservation and improvement of our forests. They should be allotted wastelands for afforestation. The paper industry should be urged to invest in regeneration, conservation and protection of forests. Moreover, the involvement of the local people, tribals and other hill and forest communities will help a lot in the conservation of our forests. Special funds must be created for the movement of forest conservation and national and corporate sector and voluntary agencies be invited to participate in it. The schemes for augmenting renewable energy sources in wastelands can also help a lot in the matter.

Social forestry should also be undertaken and encouraged on a vast scale, parallel to traditional forestry. It means involvement of the urban population in growing trees in and around the areas of their habitation. There are long and large stretches of land near towns, cities and all along the railway tracks. These waste and barren lands can be profitably used for afforestation. This would give a new impetus and dimension to our efforts of forest conservation and development of wasteland into forests. Participation of schools, colleges, trade unions, panchayats, local agencies and social organisations should be sought to make social forestry a success. ●

27. INDIAN YOUTH

INDIA'S population is more than 100 crores, out of which 40% are in the age group of 15 and 30. They form a huge reservoir of energy and cream of the country. Wisdom and discretion are not the monopoly of the elders alone. The young men and women are also intelligent and wise and much of a

nation's progress and future depend upon them. According to Samuel Johnson, "Young men have more virtue than old men; they have more generous sentiments in every respect." And in the words of Lord Byron :

> The days of our youth are the days
> of our glory;
> And the myrtle and ivy of sweet
> two and twenty
> Are worth all our laurels, though
> ever so plenty.

Young people are full of abundant energy, courage, spirit for adventure, imagination, hope and ambition. These can be very well used in constructive and developmental activities. These should not be allowed either to go waste or used for destructive purposes. The young men and women of India should be fully involved in the creative work of nation-building and reconstruction. The younger generation, which is more generous, flexible, sensitive and dynamic, can do wonders if properly guided and motivated. It is with the help of the young men and women of China that Mao Tsetung, the chairman of the People's Republic of China (1949–59) and of the Chinese Communist Party, effected the great Cultural Revolution which transformed the whole of China into one of the great political and military powers of the world. Mao was well aware of the power, exuberance, spontaneity, ebullience and unlimited energy of the youth and used these to great advantage for himself and China. Besides China, there are many other countries like France and Indonesia, etc. where the youth has helped in changing the course of history in more ways than one.

It is easy to blame the youth of India for impatience, indiscipline, irreverence for the elders, authority and social customs. But all these reflect one-sidedness and lack of proper understanding on the part of the elders and grown-ups. No doubt the youth of modern India has its own limitations and problems, etc. but these can be removed or decreased to a great extent by sympathy, understanding and appreciation. If the youth of India have any shortcomings and faults, the elders are to blame because the former mirror the latter.

Proper orientation and positive steps are needed to engage the youth of the country in nation-building activities. Their zeal, enthusiasm and energy need to be channelised in developmental activities and social reconstruction. The Indian youth, full of inexhaustible power, is always eager to do something positive, constructive and appreciable for the society and the nation.

In order to harness the youth-power of the country, a National Youth Policy has been framed to instill in the youth a deep awareness of national ideals of secularism, non-violence, integration and our ancient historical and cultural heritage. It also aims at developing qualities of discipline, self-reliance, leadership, justice, fair play, sporting spirit and scientific temper so as to enable them to combat superstitions, obscurantism and other numerous social ills and evils.

With the above objectives in view, adventure institutions, cultural centres, Yuvak Kendras, and sports centres, etc. have been established in various important cities and towns of the country. For example, Indian Mountaineering Foundation, New Delhi and National Adventure Foundation are two important institutions for promotion of adventure. These provide training facilities and financial assistance for undertaking mountaineering, hiking, trekking, expeditions, explorations, cycle-tours, etc. to promote a feeling of oneness and unity. The young men and women from one part of the country exchange visits with their counterparts from other parts It helps them to familiarise themselves with different environments, lifestyles and social customs.

Then there is the National Service Scheme (NSS). Its main objective is to involve the college and +2 level students on a voluntary and selective basis in the programme of social service and national development. Started in 1969, now it is being implemented in all the states and union territories and covers over 5,000 colleges. Under this scheme, rural and slum reconstruction, repair of roads and school-buildings, village ponds, tanks, tree plantation, conservation of environment, health and family welfare, and adult and women education, etc. are undertaken. NSS students also help local authorities in implementing various relief and rehabilitation programmes. At times of natural calamities, like floods, droughts, famines and earthquakes, NSS students and volunteers play a very important, positive and constructive role.

There are special schemes for the tribal youth to give them vocational training and to update their skills to help them in self-employment. There are youth hostels strewn all over the country to promote travel among young men and women, by providing cheap accommodation when on educational tours and excursions to historical and cultural places. The Nehru Yuvak Kendras, about 446 in number and spread all over the country, serve non-students and rural youth to improve their personality and employment capability. Under the international scouting and guiding movement, the Bharat Scouts and Guides and All India Boys Scouts Association are inculcating in the Indian youth a spirit of loyalty, patriotism and thoughtfulness for others.

But still more and vigorous efforts are needed to solve the problems of the youth. They are a frustrated lot for want of proper employment opportunities. Our education system does not take note of their requirements and, therefore, fails to prepare them well for life and career. The red-tapism, nepotism, caste considerations and favouritism further add to their problems and frustration. For want of proper leadership and ideals, they suffer from lack of direction, purpose and decisiveness. The task of tackling these and other problems of the youth is difficult and challenging but not impossible. It is the duty of the government, voluntary agencies, corporate world and the society to see that youth-power is properly harnessed, that young men and women are properly educated and trained and subsequently satisfactorily employed. The advanced and developed countries have been investing heavily for the last many decades in schemes and programmes related to the training, education, orientation and welfare of their youth.

With the passage of time, the number of young people in India is likely to increase and so it becomes imperative that more effective ways and means are found to use their vast energy in economical reconstruction and social regeneration activities. Perhaps, one of the best ways can be their greater involvement in welfare schemes, community development programmes and nation-building activities so as to generate in them a sense of purpose, pride, self-confidence and relevance. It is only by such means and efforts that the young people in India can be given the much needed self-confidence and a sense of fulfilment and belonging. They can be inspired to work in the slums, villages and hamlets in their spare time. They can be urged to adopt families, villages or clusters of houses to improve sanitation, education, social awareness, economic condition and skills of the people residing in them.

●

28. WILDLIFE PRESERVATION

INDIA'S flora and fauna is matchless. In richness, variety and abundance it has hardly any parallel. India's great latitudinal spread, encompassing a wide range of temperature conditions,

makes it rich and varied in flora and fauna. The western Himalayan region, extending from Kumaun to Kashmir, is made up of three zones — alpine, temperate and lower. The temperate zone is rich in chirpine, deodar, spruce, silver fir and forests of conifers. The alpine zone, which extends from the upper limit of the temperate zone about 4,750 metres or even higher, is characterised by high level silver fir, the silver birch and junipers. The eastern Himalayan region has about 4000 species of flowering plants, along with several varieties of palm. Many laurels, maples, alders, birch, conifers and junipers also flourish there. Rhododendrons, dwarf willows and bamboos also abound. In the Gangetic plains, forests of widely different types occur but sal forests predominate. The vegetation of Brahmaputra valley of Assam and intervening hills is luxuriant and is characterised by tall grass, broad-leaved forests and thick clumps of bamboo.

Palms of many kinds are endemic to the entire table-land of the Indian peninsula. The Malabar area, covering the west coast and the mountains of the Western Ghats, is rich in tropical vegetation. These forest areas abound in such hard wood as rose wood, iron wood, teak and also in numerous kinds of soft wood and bamboos. In the outlying islands of Andaman and Nicobar, there are a variety of forests. The number of species of flowering plants in the country is about 15,000. There are about 35,000 non-flowering plants.

The rich variety of fauna is in direct relation to the abundance and opulence of the flora. Both are inter-linked and interdependent in many ways. The flora depend on the fauna for its fertilisation, propagation and spread, while the latter's existence and survival depends on the former. There are about 350 species of mammals and 1,200 species of birds. More than 30,000 species of insects, apart from a great variety of reptiles and fishes are also found.

The mammals include the elephant, the Indian bison, Indian buffalo, the blue-bull or nilgai, four-horned antelope, black buck, Indian wild ass, the famed one-horned rhinoceros and many varieties of deer. Under the big game category come the Indian lion, the tiger, the panther, leopard and various species of smaller cats. Many types of bears roam the western Himalayas, but only a single species of panda is found. Several species of monkeys and apes are common. The wild yak inhabits the upper lands of Ladakh.

India is very rich in bird life also. The Indian peacock, with its splendid blue plumage, is the national bird. Several other species, such as ducks, pheasants, partridges, jungle fowl, quails, green pigeons, mynahs, bulbuls, parakeets, hornbills, herons, and cranes, etc. are a familiar sight. The rivers and lakes harbour crocodiles, gharials and a large variety of indigenous fish. Trout is common in hill streams and the masheer is found in most of the large rivers.

Sometimes it is asked why we should preserve wildlife and conserve forests when we ourselves need more land for agriculture, housing and industries. Moreover, it is argued that wild beasts and birds destroy our crops and gardens. The wild beasts also pose a threat to our domestic animals and livestock. Why then should there be reserved forests and sanctuaries? Why should our scarce money and resources be spent in protecting lions, tigers, musk deer, crocodiles, cranes or swans? What do we lose if some species are already extinct, and some others are on the verge of extinction?

Obviously, these questions and queries betray our ignorance and wrong priorities. Wildlife is an essential and integral part of nature. The wild birds, animals, insects and reptiles help to maintain a balance in nature and conservation of environment. God has not created them without purpose. All these species have their respective and definite roles to play in the larger scheme of things. We should not forget that man is also an animal but social, intelligent and rational. We share many things in common with them. Our kinship with them is very long and established. They are there to enrich and make our life more enjoyable and meaningful. The decrease in their numbers is bound to influence the ecology and quality of our life adversely. They are as good and essential part of nature as we are. They are a constant and renewable source of food, medicine, and protection of environment. Nothing is useless in nature. That is why they find such an important place in our art, culture, religion, literature and mythology. Without them more than half the charm of human life would be destroyed. They all are our great friends, without whom we cannot do. For example, snakes protect our crops by destroying rodents; vultures and kites, etc. do our scavenging work; lions and tigers, etc. keep the deer population in check and the birds and insects help in fertilisation of fruits, flowers and crops. Fish, deer, fowls, pheasants, rabbits, partridges, wild buffaloes, and hogs, etc. provide us meat. If there were no birds, life would be without much sweet music, colour, diversion, solace and beauty. In other words, wildlife is really precious and it is our bounden duty to preserve and protect it.

From a tourist's point of view, our wildlife is a great attraction. Foreign tourists come here to see the Royal Bengal tiger and Asiatic lion, the majestic elephant, the one-horned rhino, the colourful peacock, the wonderful birds of paradise and to angle the trout and the masheer. They help us in earning precious foreign exchange. There are many things in life which are indispensable but we are seldom conscious of their importance. This applies to wildlife as well. These birds, beasts, insects and reptiles form an integral part of nature, human life, and national wealth.

The extinction of many species of wildlife in India has sounded the warning bells. Thank God that we have not turned a deaf ear to these signals. We have the Zoological Survey of India (ZSI), with its headquarters in Kolkata and 16 regional stations spread all over, for surveying the fauna resources of the country. The Wildlife Protection Act, 1972, governs the wildlife conservation and protection of endangered species both inside and outside the forest. Under this Act, trade in rare and endangered species has been banned. It is a cognisable offence to kill these species. There are presently 75 national parks, 421 wildlife sanctuaries and 35 zoological gardens in the country, covering nearly 4.5% of the geographical area. But still much remains to be done to protect and conserve wildlife in India. ●

29. RURAL DEVELOPMENT

INDIA lives in villages. About 70% of its population lives in villages, scattered all over the country like stars in the night sky. About 96% of India's geographical area is covered by villages. The vast majority of India living in rural areas cannot be taken lightly in any planning aimed at socio-economic development of the country.

It is now increasingly being felt that no planning can be successful unless more and more attention is paid to rural development schemes and poverty alleviation programmes. Therefore, many new schemes to ameliorate the conditions of the rural population are being launched, and the old ones are being being completed expeditiously. That this rural bias and thrust has registered a success is evident from the fact that the poverty line has come down significantly, from over 57% in 1961 to 26% in 1999-2000. The implementation of various community development programmes in the first three Five Year Plans and specific poverty alleviation and unemployment removal programmes during the Fourth, Fifth, Sixth, Seventh, Eighth and Ninth Five Year Plans have gone a long way in the upliftment of the masses in the villages. The quantum of financial assistance and allocation under the Ninth Five Year Plan was raised substantially and many major structural changes have been effected to achieve the targeted goals of rural development, poverty alleviation and employment generation schemes. Consequently, the number of beneficiaries is rising rapidly. The Constitutional sanction granted to gram panchayats, etc. has further boosted the morale of rural institutions.

Integrated Rural Development Programme (IRDP) is a major instrument to alleviate rural poverty. The main objectives of IRDP are to raise families of the identified target group above the poverty line and create substantial opportunities of self-employment in the villages. The funds for this programme are shared 50 : 50 between the Centre and the states. In case of the Union Territories, complete financial assistance is provided by the Centre. The scheme is being implemented through the District Rural Development Agency (DRDA) and block level functionaries at the grass root levels. At the level of the state, there is a co-ordination committee headed by the chief secretary to look after its overall implementation. IRDP was first launched in 1978–79 in 2,300 blocks and was extended to cover all the 5,011 blocks of the country from October 2, 1980.

The scheme, meant to improve the social and economic condition of the poorest of the rural poor, is being evaluated through research conducted by independent and government institutions. According to the report of January-December 1989, about 20% of the old families crossed the poverty line of Rs. 3,500 and 28% of the revised poverty line of Rs. 6,400. However, about 78% of the families had incremental income. Nearly 34% of the assisted families belong to destitutes and 46%, very poor groups. The major impact of the scheme is that it benefits the poorest and the most deprived sectors of the society. The families eligible for help under the scheme are those where the annual family income is less than Rs. 4,800 per year. It also includes families of small and marginal farmers whose operational holding is less than 5 acres of land. The final selection of these poor families is done through gram panchayats and gramsabhas. Special attention is being paid to women. They are organised in groups for productive activities. These groups are given training and provided with suitable monetary help for increasing their family income.

Then there is the National Scheme of Training of Rural Youth for Self-Employment (TRYSEM), launched as a centrally-sponsored scheme on 15 August, 1979. The main emphasis of the scheme is on equipping rural youth, in the age group of 18–35 years, with necessary skills and technology to take up vocations for self-employment in agriculture and allied activities, industry, services and business. There are some special schemes to improve the lot of rural women and children, under which groups of 5–10 rural women are formed for carrying on income generating activities. Each group is sanctioned a revolving fund of Rs. 15,000. In case of states, the fund is shared equally by the Centre, state government and UNICEF, while in the Union Territories, the Centre bears Rs. 10,000 per group and the balance is borne by UNICEF. UNICEF also bears the expenditure on the staff component for a period of six years. The scheme has taken significant strides since its beginning in 1982.

Similarly, various pilot projects have been launched to generate employment. These include Crash Scheme for Rural Employment (CSRE), Pilot Intensive Rural Employment Programme (PIREP) and National Rural Employment Programme. These schemes and programmes specifically aim at generating additional gainful employment opportunities, creation of durable community assets and improvement of overall quality of life in the rural areas. To improve the lot of landless labourers, the Rural Landless Employment Guarantee Programme (RLEGP) was launched in 1984. The programme guarantees employment to at least one member of every landless labour family up to 100 days in a year. The Jawahar Rozgar Yojana is an ambitious programme being implemented through the village panchayats. It seeks to guarantee employment to at least one person in a rural household living below the poverty line. It was launched in 1989. Swaranjayanti Gram Swarozgar Yojana, launched in April 1999, is a new scheme for rural development.

The budget for the year 1995–96 was again a village-oriented one, in which many gifts were given to the rural masses. It envisaged establishment of Rural Infrastructure Development fund, a technological development and modernisation fund for small scale industries, with Rs.200 crores initial capital, a National Social Assistance Scheme to give a minimum old age pension and lumpsum survivor benefits to the poor and maternity benefits to poor women among many other schemes. It also proposed to set up an exclusive line of credit of Rs. 400 crores to co-operative and regional, rural banks to meet the needs of scheduled castes and tribes in a 100-odd predominantly rural, tribal districts. There is also a proposal to begin a Group Life Insurance Scheme of the LIC to be implemented by the panchayats in rural areas. The liberal package for the rural poor and vulnerable sections of the village society is laudable, but the main problem is that all the benefits do not reach the targeted poor people. Much of the funds are misappropriated by intermediaries responsible for the implementation of these packages. ●

30. SPACE RESEARCH

MAN is adventurous, intelligent and his thirst for knowledge is limitless. This insatiable thirst has urged him to probe and unravel the mysteries of space, the continuous and limitless expanse extending in all directions. Space is everywhere and all around us, an ever-expanding phenomenon. Space contains the whole universe, including all the planets, the sun, the moon, the earth, the stars and whatever there is known and unknown in the universe. The limit where the earth's atmosphere ends is called outer space. The universe and space are almost synonymous. Space is eternal, universal and ageless. It can neither be destroyed nor created. It is estimated

that observable space or universe is 25 billion light years in diamater and one light year distance means approximately 9460,000,000,000 km. It contains countless galaxies. Each and every galaxy, like our own Milky Way, is a grouping of innumerable stars. It is all so wonderful, mysterious and awe inspiring.

Man's curiosity about space and eagerness to unravel its mysteries is quite natural. Indian and world mythology and literature are full of cosmic tales, adventures and allusions. The progress in space-probe and technology during the last few decades has been spectacular and staggering. Now we have means as fast as, or faster than, sound to travel from one place to another. Consequently, the world has almost become a global village. During this period many satellites and spacecrafts have been launched for various purposes. It has revolutionised the means of mass communication, like radio, T.V. and broadcasting. It has not only enhanced our communication capabilities but also helped us in providing advanced disaster warning, search and rescue measures, distance education, and remote sensing, etc. Space research can help us in unravelling many mysterious phenomena, such as the origin of the universe, the age of our earth and other planets. It may ultimately help us in the distant future to know whether life exists on any other planet or heavenly body.

The invention of rocket was a revolutionary step in the field of space travel and research. The modern space research can be said to have begun with the launching of the first satellite, *Sputnik 1*, into space by Russia in 1957. *Sputnik 2* sent in the same year carried a dog named Laika. It successfully supplied valuable data for a week, after which the radio transmitter of the satellite suddenly stopped transmitting signals to the earth. It was a milestone in the space research programme. In 1961 Yuri Gagarin, of the then Soviet Union, became the first man to go into space and orbit round the earth. This was followed by American space launches carrying men and other living beings. In 1969, a Russian spaceship passed by the moon within a distance of about 6500 kms. Then was launched *Lunik III*, which landed on the moon. In the same year U.S.A. sent its *Ranger 7* to the moon. These were spectacular achievements heralding an era of miraculous feats in space travel, technology and research. In July 1969, Neil Armstrong became the first man to land on the moon. He was later joined by his colleague astronaut Edwin Aldrin. They reached the moon on board the spaceship *Apollo-11* and spent 21 hours on its surface, collecting rock and soil samples and then safely and triumphantly returned to the earth to the great wonder, awe and exultation of the whole world. Then again in November 1969 the American scientists repeated this feat by landing Charles Conrad, Richard Gordon and Alan Bean on the moon on board the spaceship *Apollo-12*. They returned to the earth after spending 32 hours on the moon, which is our nearest neighbour, at a distance of about 380,000 km. The Americans again landed on the moon for the third time in 1971 in their spaceship *Apollo-14*. Then *Apollo-15* landed for the fourth time on the moon.

But it was just the beginning of a brilliant saga of space travel and research. The conquest of the moon is not enough as man's search into the unknown knows no limits. And so flights to other planets began. The Americans launched

Pioneer I in March 1972 on a 21-month mission into space, past Jupiter, Saturn, Uranus, Neptune and Pluto. It was the first man-made object to travel the solar system. Since man's first landing on the moon, there have been scores of space flights by the U.S. and the then U.S.S.R., marking a beginning of a bold, new and dynamic era. In 1978, the Russian scientists sent the first international crew in space, consisting of a Russian and a Czech cosmonaut. In 1979, the Soviet cosmonauts succeeded in growing onion sprouts on board *Salyut 6*. In 1977, the U.S. launched *Voyager I* to probe the outer space and the solar system. The *Voyager II* was sent into space the same year, past the planet Saturn.

Columbia, the first space shuttle, was launched by America on April 12, 1981 and returned to the earth after 54 hours in space. Unfortunately, on February 1, 2003 *Columbia* space-shuttle exploded in mid-air, just minutes before landing while returning from a successful space voyage, killing all its crew members. *Columbia* was a multipurpose and reusable spacecraft which took-off like a rocket. It could be used both as a satellite and a glider. It was used to launch satellites, contact, retrieve, and repair spacecrafts in the orbit. The U.S. spaceship *Pioneer 10* was launched in June 1983 to travel to the stars past the planets and the sun. In 1984, the space shuttle *Challenger* became the first spaceship to retrieve and repair an ailing solar satellite in April, 1984.

The end of the Cold War has ushered in a new era of space co-operation, research and technology. It has also removed the dangers of space weapons and the star wars to a great extent. Now, the possibilities of world destruction through space weapons like missiles, etc. have receded because of this understanding between the two superpowers of the world. It ensures the use of space for peaceful purposes only, at least, for the time being.

On March 16, 1995, the *Soyuz* capsule launched by the Russians docked with the orbitting Russian space station *Mir*. This space capsule carried a U.S. astronaut, Norman Thagard. Space station *Mir* had been in orbit for 9 years but it was for the first time that an American astronaut was transported to a Russian space station in a Russian space capsule. Soon the U.S. space shuttle, *Discovery,* also docked with *Mir*. This paved the way for the proposed joint mission to Mars in the future. This co-operation in the field of space research between America and Russia is really welcome. It now seems certain that the day is not far when the combined efforts of Russia and America will achieve the goal of permanent human settlement on the moon and landing of man on Mars. Co-operation in space technology can further boost the unmanned explorations of the solar system and beyond. ●

31. INDIAN SPACE PROGRAMME

INDIAN mythology is full of stories of interplanetary travels and flights. From the very beginning of civilisation, space-flights have fired the human imagination. The modern space-age can be said to have begun with the launching of the *Sputniks* by Russia. Since then research and efforts in space travel have assumed many dimensions. The landing of man on the moon, the launch of space shuttles, and stations, etc. and the spectacular success of such spaceships as *Mir*, *Viking*, *Voyager, Galileo, Ulysses*, etc. reflect the strides taken in space by man. In the words of American President, Mr. Bush, "The infrastructure of space launch capability would be to the 21st century what the great highways and projects were to the 20th. Reliable space-launches would provide the 'highway' to solar system in the next century. We are well underway with unmanned explorations of the solar system."

India's entry into space-age is rather late but it is said that better late than never. The beginning was made in 1975, when India launched its first scientific satellite *Aryabhatta I* into space, in collaboration with the U.S.S.R. As we did not have our own rocket-launcher, we were helped by the Russians. However, it gave the country space status. The second satellite, *Bhaskara I*, was launched on 7th June, 1979 from a Soviet cosmodrome. This 444 kg experimental satellite contained instruments for carrying out remote sensing experiments. Then, an improved version of *Bhaskara I*, *Bhaskara II* was launched on 20th November, 1981, with the help of a Soviet booster-rocket. *Rohini* was the first Indian satellite to be launched from the Indian soil, using the indigenous *SLV-3* vehicle on July 18, 1980. The launch rocket took 12 minutes to put *Rohini* in its orbit round the earth. *Rohini* made a perfect take- off from Sriharikota in Andhra Pradesh. With this India became the sixth country in the world to possess satellite launching capability. The other members of the space club were the U.S.S.R., the U.S.A., France, China and Japan.

The Indian Space Research Organisation (ISRO) is responsible for the planning and execution of the space programme in India. It develops and fabricates rockets and satellites, etc. for different uses. It has its own rocket launching station at Thumba, near Thiruvananthapuram. It has a great locational advantage being very close to the magnetic equator. There is no other rocket launching station in the world close to the magnetic equator. The U.N. has recognised it as an international facility.

The Indian National Satellite System (INSAT), a multipurpose operational satellite system, was established in 1983. Since then it has successfully launched a series of INSATs including more advanced ones like *INSAT-2C*. Similarly, operational Indian Remote Sensing Satellites have made phenomenal progress. The series began with *IRS-IA* in March 1988. The *IRS-IC* had much better spectral and spatial resolutions, more frequent revisits, stereo viewing and on-board capabilities. It was followed by *IRS-ID, IRSP4*, *INSAT-3B*, *GSLV-D1* and *GSLV-D2*.

India has now deployed such Intermediate Range Ballistic Missiles (IRBM) like the *Prithvi*, *Nag*, etc., which have been very successfully tested many a time. India's ambitious plan in rocketry, space research and missile technology have opened the path for continuous space exploration and self-reliance. The success of these space efforts marks a great advancement and proof of the scientific, engineering and technological capabilities of the Indian scientists.

In the field of developing and manufacturing of space-launch vehicles, as well as components, India has been a leader among the developing countries. It has already developed Polar Satellite Launch Vehicle (PSLV) capable of launching 1000-kg class of satellites into a polar sun synchronous orbit. It will soon develop and manufacture Geosynchronous Satellite Launch Vehicle, GSLV, incorporating cryo-engine technology, capable of placing 2,500 kg INSAT class of satellites in geosynchronous transfer orbit.

The space programme in India primarily aims at providing space-based services in the areas of communication, meteorology, resources survey and management. In these areas, India has already made significant progress through a well-integrated, self-reliant programme. Indian space research has not only enhanced the communication capabilities, but now it is also being widely used for providing advanced disaster warning, search and rescue measures, and distance education in remote areas. Similarly, space remote sensing is providing vital inputs for agriculture, soil, forestry, land and water resources, environment, minerals, ocean development, and in the management of drought and flood disasters.

The wide network of space centres and units include Vikram Sarabhai Space Centre (VSSC) Thiruvananthapuram, ISRO Satellite Centre (ISAC), Bangalore, Space Application Centre (SAC), Ahmedabad, SHAR Centre Sriharikota in Andhra Pradesh, Development and Educational Communication Unit (DECU), Ahmedabad, ISRO Telemetry Tracking and Command Network (ISTRAC), Bangalore, and Master Control Facility at Hassan in Karnataka. The scientists, technologists, engineers and technicians working in these prestigious institutions ensure steady progress in the field as they are exceptionally talented, devoted and ambitious. India is sure to achieve much more, in the use of space, both for the purpose of peace and for defence.

Squadron Leader Rakesh Sharma was the first Indian to go into space. He was launched into space, aboard the Soviet spaceship *Soyuz T II* alongwith Yuri Vasilevich and Gennady Mikhailovich, the two Russian cosmonauts. It happened on 3rd April, 1984, at Baikanour cosmodrome in Kazakhastan. Thus, India became the 14th nation to have sent a man into space. Dr. Kalpana Chawla became the first Indian lady to go into space in November, 1997. She was chosen out of 2,962 applicants by Johnson Space Centre in Houston, Texas, U.S.A. The 42 year old dynamic lady had the proud and rare privilege to embark on her second space voyage on January 16, 2003. But, tragically, on her return journey aboard the space shuttle, *Columbia*, on February 1, 2003, there was an explosion minutes before landing, killing her and all the other crew members. ●

32. LAND REFORMS IN INDIA

INDIA is primarily an agricultural country and its economy is based on agriculture. India lives in villages, and in a village economy the ownership of land is of crucial importance. From the very beginning, Indian villages were self-reliant and village autonomy was an established fact. The land belonged to the village community as a whole, but during the medieval and British periods this autonomy and land-system was destroyed as zamindari system came into existence and the farmer was dispossessed of his right to the land he cultivated. Since then, he worked for others for a pittance, without owning the land. Thus, began a long period of his exploitation and isolation from the village economy, till India got independence in 1947 and some land reforms were introduced to improve the lot of the Indian farmer.

Agriculture is the backbone of Indian economy. This sector provides livelihood to about 70% of our workforce, contributes nearly 32% of Net National Product (NNP) and accounts for a sizable share of total value of the country's exports. It supplies the bulk of wage goods required by the non-agriculture sector and raw material for a large section of industry. To achieve all this, land reforms were necessary because the old agrarian system and structure was not conducive to modernisation of agriculture. Therefore, it was sought to be replaced by a more egalitarian social structure ever since the inception of the planning process.

Land reforms programme in India has been designed to remove the old, feudal socio-economic structure of rural India to provide greater fillip to modernisation of agriculture and promote agricultural productivity. It also intends to bring in the largest possible number of poor farmers and agricultural workers to the mainstream. It helps to raise the status of the weaker sections of village society. The Seventh Five Year Plan viewed the land reforms as an intrinsic part of the anti-poverty strategy. One of the chief land reforms has been the abolition of intermediary tenures. As a result, more than 200 lakh tenants have been brought into direct contact with the state. Besides, according to a government report, a large part of an estimated 60 lakh hectares of waste, fallow and other classes of land vested in the state have been distributed to the landless and marginal land-holders.

Tenancy reforms in India include legislative provisions to provide ownership rights to tenants, security of tenure to tenants, subtenants and share-croppers. Provisions regarding fixation of rents payable by the tenant and prohibition of eviction, except on specified grounds, further strive to safeguard the interests of tenant farmers. Consequently, thousands of tenants have been conferred ownership rights in respect to 153 lakh acres of land.

In conformity with national guidelines issued in 1972, the land ceiling laws were re-enacted by the states. Before this, many states had enacted land ceiling laws in the 50s and 60s and more than 9.93 lakh hectares of land was taken over by the states. Out of this, 7.5 lakh hectares were distributed to the landless poor. Till December 1992, in all, 73.76 lakh acres have been declared surplus in the old and revised ceiling laws. Out of this, 64.1 lakh acres have been taken possession of and 50.31 lakh acres have been distributed to 46.1 lakh landless agricultural labourers and other eligible persons.

The issue relating to the completion of distribution of surplus lands and all relevant aspects of land reforms and land records management were discussed at a conference of state revenue ministers held on March 14, 1992, at New Delhi, under the chairmanship of the Prime Minister. And it was decided that all available surplus land, free from encumbrances, may be distributed by 30th June, 1992, and at least 75% of the land involved in litigation in revenue courts must be freed from such litigation and distributed. In addition, certain other recommendations in regard to land records and distribution of Bhoodan land were also made. Since much of the land distributed under the ceiling laws is of poor quality, the assignees are being provided financial assistance at the rate of Rs. 2,500 per hectare.

Correct and up-to-date land records are an essential pre-condition for effective implementation of land reforms, particularly for providing security of tenure to tenants and share-croppers and for smooth flow of credit and agricultural inputs to the landholders. In some states, land and crop records are being updated periodically. They have also been computerised in a few states. A centrally sponsored scheme for revitalising revenue administration and updating the land records is being implemented to provide financial assistance to the states.

After the abolition of zamindari system some major reforms like ceiling on land holdings, tenancy reforms, and consolidation of holdings, etc. have effected a big change in the agrarian class structure and village economy but still much remains to be done. Our land reforms suffer from many lacunae and loopholes and, as the result, the net results are far from satisfactory. Land distribution among the poor and landless farmers has been tardy and cumbersome and the inter-mediaries are still there. Moreover, there have been many cases of evasion of land ceiling acts. There is a big lobby of rich and influential farmers and a huge amount of black money is at work against the land reforms and the interest of the poor, landless farmers and share-croppers. The corruption prevailing in enforcement agencies further worsens the situation. The peasants, farmers and agricultural workers are illiterate, uneducated and unorganised. The bureaucracy is indifferent to the redressal of genuine grievances of the farmers and, therefore, the progress of land reforms in India is more on paper and in reports than in reality. The effective implementation of land reforms calls for a strong political will and decisions. ●

33. VALUE OF GAMES AND SPORTS

THE value of games is now being increasingly recognised in India from personal, social, educational and national points of view. Games and sports are essential for the all round development of a personality. It is by playing games and sports that we can develop and maintain our health. Many of the modern diseases like hypertension, blood-pressure, diabetes, piles, obesity, and indigestion, etc. are the direct results of our current lifestyle, which excludes physical exercise or activity.

It is only in a sound body that a sound mind resides. Absence of games has also resulted in many mental ailments and sleeplessness.

Games keep our body alert, active, youthful and energetic. In activities involving games and sports, blood-circulation increases and there is an increased supply of oxygen. Only a healthy person can work long, hard and cheerfully. An unhealthy person may not take as much interest in work as a healthy one. Health can be maintained by exercise alone. But games and sports have some additional benefits as they are played in groups and in healthy competitive spirit. Among many other things, they help develop co-operation, quality of leadership, team spirit and a willingness to submit to, and further, the rule of law. Games instil in the players the spirit of self-reliance, justice, fair play and sporting spirit. They make people bold, adventurous, social, disciplined and more conscious of their responsibilities towards society and nation. Players have been found better equipped to fight superstitions, communalism, obscurantism and narrow approach to issues of national interest.

The kind of excitement, joy, thrill and entertainment games provide is unparalleled. They make the exercise interesting and inspire confidence in one's work. They also teach to take success and failure in one's stride, in a sporting spirit. So, games and sports have all these additional advantages which an exercise taken for physical fitness and health lacks. A player is bound to become broad-minded, tolerant, principled, disciplined, honest, more secular in his approach and tough enough to tackle problems.

It is said that, "The battle of Waterloo was won on the playing fields of Eton," because the hero of this battle was a student of this famous school. It is here, as a student and player, that he developed the great qualities of leadership, patriotism, heroism, endurance, courage, and team-spirit, etc. which later helped him in defeating Napoleon. These and other qualities of character cultivated with the help of games and sports are quite essential for success in life. They provide the much needed self-confidence and sense of fair play to the players and sports persons. They widen the mental horizon of players and make them true followers of the rule of law. A player has to follow certain rules and regulations while playing. He is penalised for a foul or transgression of the rule. He or she has to abide by the decision of the referee. He has to play in a certain place and position, under the captain or skipper of the team. One has to respect and obey their captain. Success in a game depends on co-operative team spirit and combined energetic efforts of all the members of the team. A team has to play as an organised whole in a competitive spirit, against the other team. And this goes a long way in inculcating in the players, both consciously, and unconsciously, the spirit of adventure, discipline, fair play, team spirit, co-operation and taking of quick and right decisions. A sports person may not lose his or her temper and morale even in the face of defeat because he/she would take it coolly, calmly and then would try to perform better the next time. Players know that victory and defeat are the two aspects of the same coin. There is more joy in playing than in its end result. As in games so in life, a good player will never give up or admit defeat, nor would he be demoralised by defeat. In joy and success also he will keep his cool and equipoise. The defeated players and their team congratulate the winning team, shake hands with the winning players, which teaches them to face realities of life with a smiling face in the spirit of detachment and indifference of an onlooker. Games also help in overcoming the sense of violence, arrogance and superiority as these are purged by providing them sufficient outlet.

There cannot be a better training place than a playground for our young men and women preparing to enter the fray and combat of life. It is not success or failure or the length of life that is significant. What is of utmost importance is the quality of life and the spirit in which it has been spent. In the words of poet Grantland Rice :

For when the one Great Scorer comes
To write against your name
He marks not that you won or lost
But how you played the game.

Encouragement of sports and games is also desirable as it helps in decreasing the general incidence of crimes. Games and sports develop character and give health, which are quite essential for improving the quality of one's life, acquiring wealth and success. It is because of these reasons that our government and educational institutions have become so sports-conscious and greater funds are being allocated for the promotion of sports. Sports in India is a state subject, but the Centre helps the states by rendering financial assistance and laying down guidelines for sports activities. Many states have now introduced games and sports as compulsory subjects in schools and some of them have started sports schools and sports hostels, etc. The corporate and private sector should also come forward to help promote games and sports. A beginning has been made, in the sense that many national sports events are now being sponsored by some well-known business houses, firms, companies and establishments. The business and corporate bodies should spend a percentage of their income not only in sponsoring national sports events, but also in providing playing grounds, equipment and other facilities necessary for the promotion of games and sports. ●

34. CONSTITUTION OF INDIA

CABINET Mission visited India in March, 1946 and recommended the formation of a Constituent Assembly. Accordingly, it was elected by the provincial assemblies in July of the same year. It had in all 389 members, including 93 who represented the Indian princely states. The Constituent Assembly had some eminent leaders of the country, like Jawahar Lal Nehru, Rajendra Prasad, Sardar Patel, G.B. Pant, Abul Kalam Azad, B.G. Kher, K.M. Munshi, J.B. Kriplani,

B.R. Ambedkar, S. Radhakrishnan, Liaquat Ali Khan, and Feroz Khan, etc. But Mahatma Gandhi and M.A. Jinnah were not.

The first session was held in New Delhi on 9 December, 1946. However, the Muslim League members did not participate in its deliberations. Dr. Rajendra Prasad was elected the Permanent Chairman of the Constituent Assembly. Right from inception till August 14, 1946, it held five sessions. It was declared a sovereign body according to the Indian Independence Act 1947. It made Lord Louis Mountbatten as the first Governor-General and Jawahar Lal Nehru as the first Prime Minister of Independent India. The Constituent Assembly adopted the Constitution of India on 26 November, 1949 and it came into force on 26 January, 1950.

India is a sovereign, socialist, secular, democratic republic, with a parliamentary system of government. India is governed in the terms of its Constitution. It is federal in structure, with some unitary features. The President of India is the Constitutional Head. The Constitution provides that there shall be a Council of Ministers, led by the Prime Minister, to advise the President, who shall, in exercise of his functions, act in accordance with such advice. The real executive powers are vested in the Council of Ministers and the Prime Minister as its head. They are collectively responsible to the Lok Sabha (House of the People). Similarly, in the States, the Governor is the head of the executive, but the real executive powers are vested in the Council of Ministers, with the Chief Minister as head. They are collectively responsible to the Legislative Assembly.

The Supreme Court is the highest and final judicial tribunal in India. It consists of a Chief Justice and not more than 25 other judges, all appointed by the President of India. They hold office till the age of 65. A retired judge of Supreme Court cannot practice in any court of law or before any other authority in India. The Supreme Court has both original and appellate jurisdiction. Its exclusive, original jurisdiction extends to all disputes between the Union and State or States inter se.

Besides, it has extensive original jurisdiction in regard to enforcement of Fundamental Rights guaranteed by the Constitution.

The Constitution of India embodies and enumerates an impressive list of Fundamental Rights to all its citizens, collectively and individually. These are the very cornerstones of our democracy as they ensure proper moral, material and social welfare of the people. Since these rights and freedom form an integral part of the Constitution, they cannot be violated or taken away in ordinary circumstances. These rights are : (i) The rights to equality, including equality before law, prohibition of discrimination on grounds of religion, race, sex, or place of birth and equality of opportunity in the matter of employment. (ii) The right to freedom of speech and expression, assembly, association or union, movement, residence, and the right to practice any profession or occupation. Some of these rights and freedom are subject to security of the state, friendly relations with foreign countries, public order, decency and morality. (iii) The right against exploitation, prohibiting all forms of forced labour, child labour and traffic in human beings. (iv) The right to freedom of conscious and free profession, practice and propagation of religion. (v) The right to conserve culture, language, or script and the right of minorities to establish and administer educational institutions of their choice. (vi) The right to Constitutional remedies for the enforcement of Fundamental Rights.

Indian Constitution also enumerates certain Fundamental Duties. These enjoin upon a citizen, among other things, to abide by the Constitution, to cherish and follow the noble ideals which inspired our national struggle for freedom, to defend the country and render national service when called upon to do so and to promote harmony and the spirit of common brotherhood amongst all the people of India, transcending religious, linguistic, regional and sectional diversities.

The Constitution has laid down certain Directive Principles of State Policy. These are not justiciable like the Fundamental

Rights and yet it is the duty of the State to keep these in view while enacting laws. These direct that the State shall strive to promote welfare of the people by securing and protecting as effectively as it may, a social order in which justice—social, economic and political shall inform all institutions of national life. The State shall direct the policy in such a manner as to secure the rights of all men and women to an adequate means of livelihood, equal pay for equal work and within the limits of its economy, capacity and development, to make effective provision for securing right to work, education and to public assistance in the event of employment, old age, sickness and disablement or other cases of undeserved want. The State shall also endeavour to secure to workers a living wage, humane conditions of work, a decent standard of life and full involvement of workers in the management of industries.

In the economic sphere, the State is to direct its policy in such a manner as to secure distribution of ownership and control of material resources of community to subserve the common good and to ensure that operation of economic system does not result in concentration of wealth and means of production to common detriment. Thus, these principles underline what is really desirable or what ought to be but cannot be enforced. In running the administration, these are ideals which should always be kept in view as far as possible. They all aim to take the country to the goal of peace, progress and prosperity.

The salient features of the Indian Constitution are : (i) It is right as well as flexible. (ii) It is the longest in the world. (iii) It reconciles Parliamentary sovereignty with judicial supremacy. (iv) It provides Fundamental Rights and their Constitutional remedies. (v) It proclaims that the people are sovereign. (vi) It has established parliamentary form of government. (vii) It is federal in form but unitary in spirit. (viii) It has introduced universal franchise. (ix) It incorporates Directive Principles of State Policy and Duties of the citizens. (x) It establishes independent judiciary with provisions for judicial review.

The Constitution of India provides for a single citizenship. Under the Constitution, the following categories of persons are considered as citizens of India at the commencement of the Constitution :

1. Persons born and domiciled in India.
2. Persons domiciled in the territory of India, whose parents were born in India.
3. A person who has domiciled in the territory of India and has been residing in India ordinarily for a period of at least five years.
4. Certain categories of persons who had migrated to India from Pakistan.
5. Indians who are residing abroad but who make a clear application to acquire Indian citizenship. ●

35. DEMOCRACY AND DISCIPLINE

MAN is a social being. He lives in a society, which means getting on with others. Thus, discipline is a must for getting on with others and the common welfare. There cannot be a well-organised and civilised society sans discipline. Today, we are a highly civilised, cultured and developed people only because of willing obedience to certain rules, regulations, code of conduct and social behaviour, which have been there from the dawn of civilisation. If there had been no discipline and self-imposed code of social and individual behaviour, there would not have been any civilisation, culture or progress. If these rules and regulations are not followed, there will be total chaos, bloodshed, violence, jungle rule and widespread misery. It is discipline which makes our life enjoyable, orderly, safe and worth living. Discipline forms the very warp and woof of our social fabric. Even in individual life, existence presupposes obedience of certain laws of nature.

In a democracy, discipline becomes all the more significant, for democracy is said to be the government of the people, by the people, and for the people. In this form of government, the ultimate power rests with the public and they are

sovereign. If they are not disciplined, democracy will turn into a mobocracy, a government by the crowd divided, aimless and anarchic. Democracy believes that a ballot is more powerful than a bullet, and to put this belief into practice it is necessary that people exercise self-restraint and discipline and adhere to the code of behaviour and conduct. Democracy means freedom, liberty, equality and fraternity, but it never means licence. To equate democracy with licence is totally wrong. Democracy tolerates criticism, nay invites criticism. It admits variety and grants freedom and rights. But they cannot exist without corresponding duties, obligations and rules of conduct, which constitute discipline. It is man's capacity for adjustment, equality, justice and discipline that makes democracy possible. And, at the same time, man's inclination towards indiscipline, discrimination, licence and injustice make democracy a necessity.

Democracy means an intense awareness of both, one's rights and duties. Right enjoyment of one's freedom, rights, privileges and liberties means doing things in such a manner that it does not in any way interfere with the enjoyment of these by others. There cannot be any personal freedom without social order. They go hand in hand. An indisciplined nation can degenerate into anarchy from democracy. Democracy involves a lot of self-discipline, accommodation, adjustment and compromises so that others may also enjoy the same liberty as ourselves. It is this sense of duty and discipline that makes democracy a success. A disciplined nation can face any challenge, and overcome any crisis of any magnitude. Discipline knows no exception. It is binding on all the citizens, whether one occupies the highest public office or the most humble one. All are equal before the law, the very expression of discipline.

Discipline can be said to be the very life-blood of a democratic society. No democracy in the world has ever succeeded without discipline and observance of certain rules and regulations based on morality, social ethics and norms of equality. Success of any democracy is always in direct proportion to the degree and quality of the discipline observed and maintained by its citizens. There is always a wide network of law-enforcing agencies in a democratic set-up, but self-imposed discipline is the best.

It is democracy that grants the greatest number of liberties to its citizens. The genuineness of these rights and liberties is the real test of a democracy since these are the highly cherished privileges. Without these, it would amount to a meaningless existence. These imply freedom of movement, occupation, choice, possession, work, speech, and expression, etc. At the same time, these cannot be absolute in the sense that one's freedom should not clash with that of others. Others have the same right to enjoy their freedom as we do. If there is a clash and conflict between individual freedom and that of others, democracy would be in peril and there would be no freedom at all. That is where discipline, accommodation and adjustment come in the picture. Freedom has no meaning sans society; it is the society that gives meaning and fulfilment to individual freedom and liberty. Obviously, restraint or discipline and liberty are complimentary. Without the existence of one, the existence of the other is impossible.

Democracy, which stands for equality, justice and fraternity, is desirable and it makes discipline indispensable. Indiscipline and non-observance of rules and regulations is a sure sign of decay, death and degeneration of democracy. Democracy and discipline reinforce and vitalise each other, for both have their roots in a keen awareness of one's duties, responsibility and accountability. When one is endangered, the other is automatically at the brink of destruction. A fine balance has to be struck and maintained between the two. There should not be an overdue emphasis either on discipline or liberty, because they are like the two aspects of the same coin. You cannot possess one while dispensing with the other. Violation of rules and regulations is the worst enemy of democracy. Rules and their observance is good for democracy and for the people under it. Even the oceans have their boundaries and limits. They are not unlimited and boundless and this fact gives them a definite identity, existence, and strength. Then how can we think of individual liberty without certain amount of restraints? Democracy and the rule of the law or discipline are almost synonymous. Without imbibing the spirit of discipline it is not possible to have a genuine democracy. India is the largest democracy in the world, with a population of over a billion and a successful journey of over half a century behind it. It has been possible only because the people of India are by and large law-abiding and self-disciplined; the electorate is enlightened and mature and its citizens have the capacity to judge and analyze facts to reach desired conclusions. We would not have been successful in our struggle for freedom had we been indisciplined. We showed a remarkable sense of restraint and discipline and that is why we won our freedom under the dynamic leadership of Mahatma Gandhi. It only goes to show that the foundations of Indian democracy are well laid on the rocks of self-restraint, discipline and the sense of social and moral responsibilities. It is this deep sense of duty and obligation that gives meaning to our democracy and also ensures its glorious future. ●

36. PLANNING IN INDIA

THE history of planning in India goes back to 1950, when the Planning Commission was set up to prepare the blueprint of national development. Inspired by socialistic patterns of development in the then Soviet Union, planning in India derives its objectives and social premises from the Directive Principles of State Policy incorporated in the Constitution. India adopted planning as an instrument of economic reconstruction and social development through greater private and public investment. The need for a planned development was felt all the more because of its rapidly increasing population and the widespread, appalling poverty left behind as a legacy of the foreign rule. It was felt that in a huge democratic country like India, where the Constitution has promised an egalitarian society and a welfare state, the accelerated economic growth could be achieved only through proper planning and execution. The leaders of the country, therefore, decided to strive for planned development and progress in agricultural and industrial sectors on democratic lines.

The First Five Year Plan (1951–56) aimed at an all-round development through increase in national income and improvement in living standards of the people. There were inflationary pressures and large scale imports of foodgrains. Therefore, the main thrust of the Plan was improvement of agriculture, irrigation facilities, power projects and transportation. It also aimed at enhancing the rate of investment from 5% to 7% of the national income.

The Second Plan, launched in 1956, sought an increase of 25% in national income, rapid industrialisation of heavy industries and large expansion of employment opportunities. It also sought to reduce inequalities in income and wealth and more even distribution of economic power in order to establish a socialistic pattern of society.

The Third Plan (1961–1966) was an ambitious one, which aimed at self-sustaining growth and economy. Therefore, highest priority was given to expansion of basic industries, like steel, chemicals, fuel and power, and achievement of self-sufficiency in foodgrains through greater agricultural production and utilisation of human resources to the maximum. It also sought to establish greater equality of opportunities and bring about reduction in disparities of income and distribution of national wealth. The Indo-Pak conflict in 1965, two successive and severe droughts, devaluation of rupee, steep rise in prices, along with paucity of funds added to the discomfort of our planners and so there was much delay in the implementation of the Plan. The size of development outlay also had to be kept considerably down and greater dependence on foreign aid became a necessity.

The Fourth Plan (1969-74) officially commenced on April 1, 1969, with the publication of the draft plan. Growth with stability was the main objective of the Plan.

Formulated against the backdrop of severe inflationary pressures, it aimed at an annual growth rate of 5.5% in national income through self-sufficiency in foodgrains and agricultural produce. Priority was also given to bringing inflation under control, alleviation of poverty and improvement of living standards of the people.

The Fifth Plan draft, as originally drawn up, was part of a long term Perspective Plan covering a period of 10 years from 1974–86. The new slogan was *Garibi Hatao*. By the time the Plan got its approval from the National Development Council (Sept. 1976), its premises had become obsolete. With the Janata Party coming into power in another six months, it was scrapped unceremoniously. A Rolling Plan started with an Annual Plan for 1978-79.

By the time the Sixth Plan was launched in 1980, the planners had gained much experience and expertise. They wanted result-oriented planning, aimed at accelerated growth and development in industries and agriculture through the strengthening of infrastructure. The removal of poverty and generation of greater employment opportunities were given the highest priority. It also sought greater involvement and participation of the people in formulation and implementation of various developmental schemes at different local levels. The new 20-point programme was also introduced during this period in order to benefit the unorganised sector and meet the minimum basic needs of the people.

The main objectives of the Seventh Plan were rapid growth in foodgrains, modernisation of industries, self-reliance, justice and greater employment opportunities. During the plan period, foodgrain production grew by 2.23% as compared to a long term growth rate of 2.68% during 1967–68 and a growth rate of 2.55% in the eighties. A special programme like Jawahar Rozgar Yojana was also introduced in addition to some other already existing programmes, to generate more employment opportunities and reduce the incidence of poverty among the rural population. Due recognition was also accorded to the role of small scale and food-processing industries in national development and poverty alleviation.

The Eighth Plan (1992–97) proposed a growth rate of 5.6% per annum on an average. Integrative in nature, the Eighth Plan gave priority to the rapid growth of infrastructure including power, transport and communication. In order to correct the fiscal imbalances from which the previous Plans suffered, greater emphasis was laid on higher resource mobilisation and improvement in performance of public sector units so as to avoid the debt-trap. It also aimed at devolution of power to the people's organisations at the district, block and village levels so that Panchayats, Gramsabhas and Nagarpalikas could play greater roles in the formulation and implementation of the developmental projects in their areas. With sufficient scope for change, innovation and adjustment, the Eighth Plan laid special emphasis on employment and improvement of living standards of the rural poor. The Plan also recognised "human development" as the core of all developmental efforts and gave due importance to achievement of goals in the areas of health, literacy and basic needs, including drinking water, housing and welfare activities of the weaker sections.

The broad objectives of the Ninth Five-Year Plan (1997-2002) were (i) Priority to agriculture and rural development to generate more employment and remove poverty; (ii) Accelerating growth rate with stable prices; (iii) Ensuring food and nutritional security for the poor; (iv) Providing minimum services of safe drinking water, primary health care, universal primary education and shelter (v) Checking growth of population; (vi) Empowerment of women and weaker sections of society; and (vii) Strengthening efforts to build self-reliance.

The priorities of the Ten Five-Year Plan (2002-2007) are as follows—(i) Improving the quality of life through better health and educational facilities and improved levels of consumption, (ii) Reduction in inequality.

The analysis and assessment of the above Plans clearly shows that planning as an instrument of growth and development has helped us a lot in achieving our objectives to a great extent. There have been many shortcomings and failures and yet the importance of planning and its implementation cannot be overlooked. During these four decades of planning, there have been significant achievements in the field of industries and agricultural growth, expansion of business and finance, rural development, poverty alleviation, generation of employment opportunities and improvement in standards of living of the people. There has been a determined and marked effort towards all round development of the society and the results have not been disappointing only because of the planning and its implementation. It has opened the avenues for a new and bold economic and social order based on equality and social justice, and commitment. The planning concept in India is the concept of economic growth with social justice.

●

37. ENERGY CRISIS

ENERGY is the motive power that keeps the wheels moving and other things live and dynamic. Energy forms the foundation of all our industrial, agricultural and developmental activities. Life itself is energy based. Energy is crucial for all our growth and development. There are a number of sources of energy, such as fossil fuel, wind, water and the sun. Fossil fuel has been the conventional source of our energy needs and under it come coal, lignite, petroleum and natural gas. Another source of traditional energy is fuelwood, animal waste and agricultural residues but these are known as non-commercial fuels. Unfortunately, the sources of conventional energy are depleting quite quickly. These conventional and natural sources of energy are not sufficient to meet our ever-increasing demand and, as a result, there is a crisis.

As a developing country, India needs more and more energy as it is the main input in economic and industrial development. Energy is consumed by all sectors of economy and all sections of society in India. Energy crisis is not confined to India alone. Even the developed countries like the U.S., Russia, Germany, and Japan, etc. have this problem. There is a direct and close relation between the availability of energy and the growth of a country. In spite of 42-fold increase in generation of electricity, 6-fold increase in coal-production and 130-fold increase in production of crude in India during the last four decades, there is a major shortage of energy and the gap between availability and demand is widening.

India has to import a significant portion of its oil needs. During 1992-93, our import bill for petroleum and petroleum products was nearly Rs. 17,100 crores, which rose to a staggering Rs. 71,500 crores in 2000-01. In spite of the phenomenal growth in our petroleum industry, we have to import a huge quantity of crude oil and petroleum products from other countries. The industry has witnessed tremendous progress in the field of oil-exploration and production, refining and marketing petroleum products. Domestic crude oil production reached the peak level of 330 lakh tonnes in 1990–91. However, it came down to 303 lakh tonnes during 1991–92 but it rose again, after remedial measures, to approximately 327 lakh tonnes in 1999-2000. The constant increase in prices of oil in the international market since 1973 has worsened the energy crisis in India. It has put tremendous strain on our developing economy and there is an urgent need of energy-efficient machines and devices, particularly automobiles, because transport sector is the main consumer of petroleum products. In the context of energy crisis and the ever-increasing oil import bill, high priority should be given to conservation of oil and petroleum products in transport, industrial, agricultural and household sectors. Besides, efforts to increase the indigenous production of crude oil should be intensified and private and international oil companies should be involved.

Electricity is the most popular form of energy and its demand in the country has been growing at a faster rate than other forms of conventional energy. In spite of phenomenal growth of power generation in India during the last couple of years, there is an acute shortage. Electricity plays a very vital role in both industrial and agricultural sectors. The increasing consumption of power in the country reflects our growth and development. The per capita power consumption in India is very low in comparison to other countries. The total public sector Ninth Plan outlay for power was Rs. 223,050 crore. But this outlay was insufficient in the context of our energy needs and exploitation of our thermal and hydel power potential.

Power generation requires huge funds. Establishment of new power-plants and maintenance, renovation and modernisation of existing and old ones is not possible by the state-owned state electricity boards, etc. Moreover, the transmission and distribution of power also involves huge funds and risks. The government does not have sufficient resources to meet the challenge. Therefore, it is desirable that power sector should be thrown open for private participation. It is in the fitness of things that private companies have undertaken the task in some parts of the country. The position of power shortage in the coming years appears alarming and it needs huge resources to build up the additional capacities. Not more than 20,000 MW worth capacity addition was expected by the end of the Eighth Plan, against the targeted 30,538 MW. The requirement of capacity addition in the Ninth Plan was 57,000 MW. Therefore, the private sector participation is one of the most realistic options for augmenting the power generating capacity. In 1999-2000 (April-November), 313.8 billion KW of power was generated but still power shortages continued due to gross mismanagement at all levels.

A study by the World Bank team rightly suggested the privatisation of State Electricity Boards (SEBs) as the best way to strengthen the power sector in the country. The study report said that quick completion of planned corporatisation of generation, transmission and distribution was necessary as the first step to make the restructuring process successful.

There is vast scope and many opportunities in the emerging power sector for private companies. They should come forward and set up power projects and earn huge profits. It is in this background that as many as 114 MOUs with private sector power developers have been finalised by different states, reflecting an additional capacity of 52,000 MW and an investment of over Rs. 200,000 crores. A bulk of this will be in thermal plants, where equipment accounts for 60% of the cost.

Nuclear, solar, wind and bio-gas energy can be the alternative sources of our power needs. There are four atomic power stations in India. Generation of electricity from nuclear energy commenced in 1969, with the commissioning of Tarapur Atomic Power Station, consisting of two enriched uranium fuelled boiling water reactors of 210 MW capacity each. The Rajasthan Atomic Power Station, using natural uranium as fuel, attained criticality in December 1972. The Kalapakkam Atomic Power Station, Chennai started commercial production on 21st March, 1986. These were the first sectors to be indigenously designed and constructed. This was followed by two more sectors, one at Narora in Uttar Pradesh and another at Kakrapar, Gujarat. Further expansion in nuclear power generation capacity is also in progress. India's commitment to use nuclear energy only for peaceful and economical developmental activities is well known. Thus, exploitation of nuclear energy offers an important supplement to our conventional sources of energy, in spite of considerable concern since the Chernobyl accident in the erstwhile U.S.S.R.

Modern science, technology, research and development have to play a vital role in creating and developing new and renewable sources of energy in the country. The use of non-conventional sources of energy, like wind, tidal waves, biogas and solar energy in India, are limited to non-commercial and small domestic purposes so far. But soon tidal waves wind and solar energy may be exploited for commercial purposes as well. These renewable, non-conventional sources of energy hold out a major promise to overcome energy crisis in India. Since tidal wave resources are limited only to a few coastal regions, greater emphasis should be laid on harnessing wind power, solar energy and development of biogas and biomass projects. Biogas can be increasingly used as cooking fuel in villages and towns since it is cheap, clean and convenient It can also be used for lighting and running small motors for providing power to cottage industries. The slurry from biogas is also an enriched manure. Solar energy in India holds great promise as a source of clean, convenient cheap and renewable source of energy. It is estimated that total solar insolation falling on one square metre surface, horizontal to the sun, is quite high in the country. For a greater part of the year during the day, there is much and bright sunshine throughout the country It can be used to our great advantage, to produce energy for domestic and industrial use. The day is not far away when India will be one of the leading nations of the world to tap solar energy to overcome the crisis in power generation. ●

38. CABLE AND SATELLITE TELEVISION

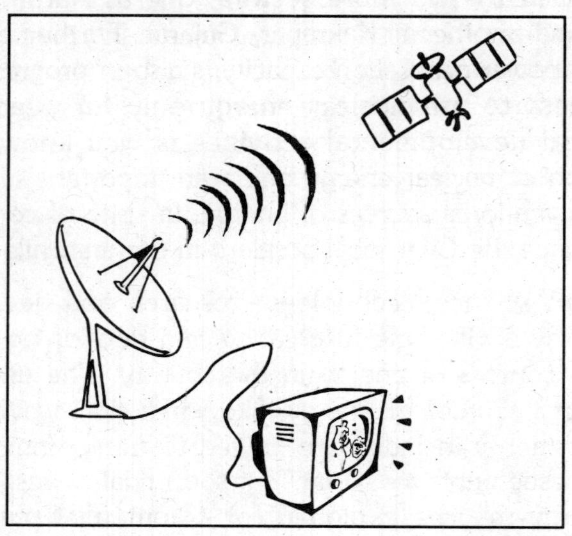

COMMERCIAL satellites have revolutionised broadcasting in India. The vast emerging market of T.V. viewers has attracted many foreign satellite companies to the country. Due to the dozens of channels that are available today, thousands of Indian families are now enjoying interesting, educative and thrilling T.V. programmes. Viewers have a very wide choice and can select a programme of their liking at any time of the day and night. There is Sony, Jain T.V., CNN, Star T.V., Zee T.V., P.T.V., A.T.V., B.B.C., and M.T.V. etc. for the viewers to switch on and enjoy their leisure hours. The cable T.V. system, based on satellite transmission, has visually invaded the homes and lives of millions of viewers, who can be seen glued to their idiot boxes, spending long and late hours. The viewing of cable T.V. programmes has become all pervasive.

Satellite and cable television cater to different tastes, and so, people of all ages and categories—young, old, children, men, women, rural folk and urbanites have great fascination for it. Sports, music, films, different types of serials have specialised programmes. M.T.V., Channel V, and Zee Music etc. have become a craze among young people because of their scintillating music, flashes of bright colour, rhythmic body-movements, attractive clothing, hi-tech musical instruments and electrifying, exotic and extravagant scenes. Cable-viewing has become almost infectious because many of the programmes are quite spicy, provocative, inviting and gratifying. This invasion from the skies has taken the cities and towns by storm and the common viewers seem to be overwhelmed.

But the cable boom and satellite system has taken its toll on studies, rest and sleep, social life, friendly gatherings and the joys of conversation. Children and adolescents shun schoolwork, studies and games to watch their favourite films, serials, and songs on television. It disturbs the viewers' work schedule and hours of sleep because of long and late hours of watching T.V. All this has adverse effect in terms of mental-poise, sound and sufficient sleep, productivity, efficiency, and tolerance, etc. This passive and pervasive entertainment is likely to create many more complexities yet not gauged and diagnosed.

In view of the growing popularity of satellite and cable T.V., and the ever-expanding market, many new satellite companies have joined the race. Among them is the U.S. Panam Sat, which launched its PAS-4 satellite in 1995. Other global companies in the fray are : Intersputnik of Russia, with its Express satellite series, Japan's JCSAT, Malaysia's Measat and Thailand's Thaicom. PAS-4, billed as the hot bird of the Asian skies, has 16 C-band transponders, requiring large dish antennae and 11 powerful KU-band transponders requiring small dishes to allow direct-to-home broadcast. It is a strong rival of Ruport Murdoch's Asiasat. The Doordarshan uses two transponders of PAS-4 for its international broadcast. One of these two transponders is meant to beam programmes to the U.S. and the second to the U.K.

The Russian Express series is a new generation satellite. The first express satellite was launched in October 1994. Many satellite T.V. channels in India are linked to the Russian Express series. All these indicate the steady increase in the popularity of satellite T.V. ●

39. COMPUTER APPLICATIONS

LIGHTNING speed, superb accuracy, high reliability, and unmatched integrity, etc. are some of the characteristics of a computer which has made its application so pervasive. There is hardly any field of human activity where it is not present today. It has revolutionised the knowledge and information processing system. Knowledge is power and so the 'chip' has become a mighty thing. It has been rightly observed that, "The fifth generation of computers is the largest battleground of the last century. It will determine a new balance of power in the world."

This tireless and marvellous machine, man's wonderful brain-child, can perform a number of complicated calculations instantly. A computer can execute over a million instructions per second and that too as many times as you like and without any mistake. Recently, an intelligent machine called Genius-2, capable of executing 166 million instructions per second, defeated the Russian Grand Master Gary Kasparov in a game of chess. The global revolution, ushered in by computers, is far more powerful than any other the world has seen so far. More miraculous than the mythical Aladdin's lamp, the computer itself has passed through an evolutionary process before it reached the present stage. But this process is continuous and millions of dollars are being spent every year in research and development to make it more perfect, versatile and user-friendly. A few years back, personal computers were used as glorified typewriters. Then they began to be linked together in a local area network (LAN). And then, equipped with telephone modems, they began to 'talk' to one another anywhere across the world. The use of modems is increasing by leaps and bounds. The world's number one software company, Microsoft, is spending about 200 million dollars every year on developing user-friendly software, for solutions ranging from video-on-demand to information search in the network.

The computer stores an ocean of information and knowledge, analyses it, retrieves information and gives results as and when ordered. It has helped in overcoming many difficult problems of multiple calculations, scientific data processing, record-keeping and industrial complications. It has proved a matchless friend and servant of science, technology and industry. Now, computing and networking has become as convenient and universal as the use of the telephone. It connects people and supplies desired information instantly so as to enable them to act on it anytime, anywhere. The speed, the accuracy, the reliability, the integrity and the security being provided by it are really staggering and stupendous.

The coming computers are likely to be still faster, convenient, handy and more sophisticated and complex. The Fortran IV, which was considered then as ultimate, has now been left far behind by more sophisticated languages. Each new generation of computers has been smaller, lighter, faster and more powerful than the one before. The next wave of these intelligent machines will further revolutionise the use of computers. Now, notebook-sized pocket computers are a common thing. For example, now you can use your laptop or

Notebook computer to hook into any phone outlet and attach to networks at home, exchange, e-mail, and voice mail, etc. Consequently, the world has turned into a global village and people have become more mobile, active and result-oriented. Independent of place, now work and business have become an activity in the real sense of the term. "Pervasive computing has great potential to redefine personal and organisational productivity. As applications become more intuitive and powerful, we all will become more productive and efficient."

The use of computers has made the complicated industrial, scientific and technological operations and their related problems easy to solve. Computerisation in offices, banks, business establishments, shops, and factories, etc. has proved a great boon in terms of accuracy, precision, costs, efficiency, reliability, speed, time, security and energy. But it has certainly increased and added to the problem of unemployment. A computer can replace scores of skilled and efficient people. In spite of this problem, computers are going to stay forever. They have become a necessity. India is computerising very fast. The spurt in the use of these miracle machines in various places, like railways, airlines, banks, defence services, business organisations, offices, research establishments, postal and communication departments is breathtaking. The computer industry, both software and hardware, has a very bright future. The government is trying its best to encourage it so that it can compete effectively with world players and contribute generously to the growth and development of the national wealth and well-being. Consequently, on the export front, the industry has shown remarkable achievements. Many computer companies, in collaboration with foreign giants in the field, have come into existence and are faring excellently. A few of them are exporting these indigenously produced machines to various developed and developing countries of the world.

These high-speed data processing and networking machines have made their presence felt in India in a big way They have been introduced in schools and colleges. Their application and use in various fields, like commercialisation, business, financing, meteorology, education, defence, research, engineering, designing, medical science, and stock-broking, etc. has now become a must. In defence, they help radar, missile and rocket launching, automatic flight, etc. Railways, airlines and hotels now offer instant information on bookings and reservations with the help of computers. They have reduced distances as they can be used to co-ordinate activities at different places. They have opened up new avenues, making shopping, entertainment, and advertising etc. interactive. They have helped in remote access to bank accounts, vital information, e-mail, paging, voice-messaging, and video-shopping.

Computing is becoming more and more pervasive. It has revolutionised teaching and learning Computers have proved very useful as simulators for training in various fields. Now, a person desirous of learning to fly an aeroplane can do so on simulators, without any risk and then finally take up actual flying. Computers can play chess, compose music, draw figures, paint, write poetry and novels and can also help in producing books in Braille for the blind. They have made trading on stock exchanges far more transparent, reliable, efficient, instantaneous, easy, fair and enjoyable. Now, through the computer terminal screen, an investor can find out the price and the quantity of scrips available. He can also find out at what time his order is executed and at what price, and what is the brokerage. Computerised trading also ensures that a seller gets the best price available in the market at any given time. It eliminates the monopoly of the jobbers and malpractices of the brokers.

The fear that one day computers will supersede the human mind is not based on facts. In spite of radical and marvellous development in computer hardware and software technology, it will only remain a machine, a handmaid of man. It can never usurp the place and position of the human brain, let alone the wisdom and sensitivity. It can never attain the creativity and thinking of the human mind. After all a computer is a machine, a product of human intelligence, which depends on human consciousness for its manufacture, maintenance, and operation. Experts opine that the chip can never overtake the cranium. They say that, "Even a decade or two from now, you will still be able to pat the latest and the biggest computers, and whisper, 'You poor dumb beast'." The most powerful computer is your brain and that is not going to change. Even the latest computer memories have no more than 100 transistors. In contrast, the number of nerve cells in your brain is as large as ten raised to the power of eleven neurons. Each of these inter-connected cells make the brain's nerve network a billion times greater than the most powerful computers being built today.

But computers have brought their problems. They can commit mistakes and when they do, they create many problems. Their mistakes are really blunders and more risky than those committed by men. They have their own virus, and they can become its victims. So much dependence on computers makes men mentally weak and passive. But the advantages far outweigh these few disadvantages. ●

40. PEACEKEEPING OPERATIONS OF THE U.N.

THE United Nations Organisation (UNO) was born out of a desire of the world leaders to save the succeeding generations from the scourge of war. But, unfortunately, soon it faced the ominous Cold War triggered by the rivalry, distrust and egoism of the two super powers, the U.S.A. and the U.S.S.R. It divided the whole world into two blocs and marked the beginning of an unprecedented race for weapons of mass destruction and stockpiling of nuclear armaments. The U.N. was reduced to a silent and helpless spectator.Actually the world has never been totally free of conflicts, battles, strifes and wars in some form or the other. The shadows of conflict have always lingered in one part of the world or another. Now the world is plagued with conflicts and conflagrations in Afghanistan, Iraq, Somalia, Rwanda, and Burundi, etc. There is instability in some of the former Soviet Republics, and Balkans. etc. In many other parts and pockets of the globe also there are aggressions, violations of human rights, acts of terrorism and peace is really in danger in spite of the end of the Cold War. It is an irony that man wants peace but is ever engaged in acts of war with himself and with others. However, it would be a real tragedy if the U.N. meets the same fate as its predecessor, the League of Nations.

In spite of the failures, setbacks and shortcomings, the achievements of the U.N., in regard to its major aims, have not been insignificant. When this world body was formed formally on 24th October, 1945, it set itself the following aims and objectives:

(i) To maintain international peace and security through collective efforts for the prevention of threats to peace and for the suppression of aggression.

(ii) To bring about peaceful resolution of settlement of international disputes.

(iii) To promote the process of self-determination of peoples or decolonisation.

(iv) To help achieve international co-operation in social, economic, cultural and human fields. It also aims at disarmament and the establishment of New International Economy.

The membership of U.N. is open to all peace-loving countries who believe in the above aims and objectives of the organisation. It has been divided into six main organs for its smooth functioning and obtaining of the above objects. These organs include—

(i) General Assembly
(ii) Security Council
(iii) Secretariat
(iv) Economic and Social Council
(v) Trusteeship Council, and
(vi) International Court of Justice.

It is the main responsibility of the Security Council to maintain peace and security in the world. It has 15 members, out of which the United States, Britain, China, France and Russia are permanent members. The other ten non-permanent members are selected by the General Assembly, by two-third majority for a period of two years. It is presided over on a monthly basis by its member states, in alphabetical order. Each member has one vote but on vital issues all 5 permanent members must vote 'yes' if the resolution is to be passed. Since each permanent member-state has a veto power, no decision can be taken and implemented unless passed unanimously. Whenever there is a complaint before it, the Council tries to settle the matter through negotiations between the concerned member states. If this does not succeed, the Council can take other appropriate measures, including despatch of U.N. troops, which are supplied by the member-states to remove the aggression and maintain peace and security in the given region.

Many times, the veto power of the permanent members of the Council has been a hurdle in the constructive, impartial and effective approach to crucial problems. Moreover, the permanent membership being limited to the 5 state members cannot be justified at all. To make it more representative and democratic, countries like India, Mexico, and Japan, etc. should be given permanent berths and the number of non-permanent members should be increased considerably. Its present structure makes it, more or less, a club of the few exclusive nations, resulting in a sure tilt in their favour. It has been successful in matters where the interests of none of these powers have been directly or indirectly involved. Due to this defective structural and operational design, the Council has failed many times to resolve a conflict and exercise its moral authority against the aggressor. It failed to play a positive and desired role in the Cuban crisis (1962), the Hungarian crisis (1956), the long-drawn out Vietnam war, Afghanistan, Bosnia, Burundi, Rwanda, and Iraq etc. But at the same time its successful action in Korea (1950), its success in the withdrawal of foreign forces from Suez Canal (1956), its installation of the U.N. forces in the Gaza Strip and the Gulf of Aquaba (1957), and implementation of ceasefire in Kashmir (1948), etc. should not be lost sight of. Obviously, its achievements in respect of its peace-keeping operations have been of a mixed type and it cannot be denied that the U.N. has been a centre of quiet diplomacy and exchange of views to resolve tension among the member nations to some extent. But there is no room for complacency and desirable structural and operational changes must be effected to make it a more effective instrument of harmony, peace, co-operation and genuine disarmament.

Recently, the peacekeeping of the U.N. has been under much pressure because the U.S.A. has cut its contribution to the U.N. peacekeeping operations. And the U.S. President is helpless in the matter because he cannot send his forces on such missions without the consent of the Congress. The U.S.-initiated peace operations in Somalia failed only because they lacked the full backing of the Congress. Moreover, the U.S. was also not willing to let other nations run the operations. The U.S. contributes about 32% of the costs of the U.N. peacekeeping operations and it has been proposed to be slashed down to 25%, while the Congress wants to bring it further down to 20%.

But it is heartening to note that Japan, who is next to America in contributing towards the cost of U.N. peacekeeping operations, now wants to play a more prominent role in the matter, and it is willing to dispatch its troops for the purpose.

The U.N. has been a means and an instrument to maintain peace and harmony and to avoid conflicts, but it is not an end in itself. Without this instrument the world would not have been as orderly and peaceful as it is today. It has certainly contained many small conflagrations from flaring up and becoming big. Within its limitations, and the circumspection imposed by the personal interests of its permanent members of the Security Council, the U.N. has been instrumental in eliminating the Cold

War and the prospects of a third world war. Gradually, in the wake of the end of Cold War, the U.N. is moving to the centrestage and increasingly playing a significant role, directly or indirectly, in shaping events of the world to promote peace, harmony and protection of human rights. ●

41. FASHIONS

IT is said that you cannot dip your finger twice in the same river. It underscores the law of change and flux. Fashions are no exception to this law. They come and go and change rapidly with the spirit of times. Fashions come into vogue and then go out because man loves change, variety and novelty. Old, routine, stereotyped, stale and typecast things are not to his liking. With the change in the mood of man, change in styles, manners, conduct and way of life also come about. It adds zest and liveliness to life. Change and variety is the other name of fashion. Fashions are infectious as well and spread rapidly like wildfire, especially among young men and women in big towns and cities. Youth is more fashion-conscious because they represent life in terms of energy, courage, expectations, potentialities, power, and vigour. They want to look smart, upto-date, charming and fresh in their dress, etiquette, styles of shoes, and hair-do, etc. They want to enjoy every moment of life and are full of unlimited zeal and appetite for it.

By nature, man is fashionable because of his inherent desire to see and to be seen. New and current styles in clothes and manners, etc. help people in becoming more smart, attractive, fascinating and lovable. People never like to be out of fashion. Fashion is not confined to etiquette, manners, dresses alone. It is pervasive and even religion, literature, and arts, etc. have their own fads and fashions. For example, the thirst for fashion has given rise to a variety of styles in writing and there are as many styles as there are famous writers, authors and poets.

Fashions can also be abused as well and become harmful when turned into an obsession. Then they mean waste of time, energy, and money. It is better to be a little out of fashion than to be in fashion at the cost of one's conscience and discretion.

Young men and women living in big towns and cities, with a network of fast and effective means of communication and availability of audio-visual aids in plenty, are really fashionable people. In the urban areas, thousands of people live and mix with each other and exchange ideas, opinions and interact freely. They belong to different classes, faiths, and speak different languages and, therefore, have different manners, tastes and styles. There are clubs, societies, social gatherings and get-togethers, which bring people into close contact with one another. Then there are hotels, restaurants, cinema halls, colleges, universities, schools, and offices, etc. where people see different styles and fashions and then try to imitate or to improve upon the existing ones. Fashion-consciousness in cities is so widespread and deep that as soon as a fashion comes in vogue in London, Paris, New York, Berlin or Rome, it is adopted and patronised by people in India. The means of communication are now so fast that the earth has turned into a global village and the infectious fashion knows no boundaries of time and space. The people in villages, rural areas and remote places remain untouched by the waves of fashion, both, because of lack of means of communication and poverty. But villages and towns too are not immune as traditional values, modes of living and traditions are giving way to change and novelty. To some extent, they too are affected by new fashions, designs, patterns and way of living and as the process is slow and gradual, it takes time for a fashion to reach the villages from the cities through films, videos and personal contacts.

Films and cable T.V. are a great source of fashions and quick changes in trends. Fashions are liquid and changeable like weather. Till recently, bell-bottoms, midis, minis and maxis were quite in fashion and now they are out of fashion. Again tight-bottoms, skirt-tops, salwar-kamiz and saris are in fashion. But fashion is unpredictable and keeps on changing according to the moods, fancies and ideas of the people and the influence of the popular films. Therefore, it is not easy to predict what is fashionable. Fashions are also influenced by glossy, colourful and eye-catching textile advertisements, fashion shows, propaganda of fashion and dress designers, articles in the fashion magazines and foreign visitors.

Now, people spend a good amount of their pocket money and earnings to keep themselves in fashion. They are very particular about their dress, hairstyle, cosmetics, shoes, ornaments and manners. Has not Shakespeare declared in Hamlet, "the apparel oft proclaims the man". Therefore, urbanites, particularly young men and women always keep themselves abreast of modern trends in styles and fashions. Consequently, the tailors, fashion designers, cosmetic manufacturers have a booming business. They catch on the new ideas in circulation and immediately push fashion products to suit the new fads, fashions and thoughts. Fashion designing and technology is now an established branch of human knowledge, science and practice. It provides employment and business to millions of people throughout the world and there has been a huge investment in the fashion industry. Expert fashion-designers, technologists, tailors and drapers are busy day and night to cater to the needs of the fashion-conscious in society. They not only cater to the tastes of the people but also create taste and fashion and thereby earn huge profits.

Freedom is man's most cherished possession and the freedom to choose one's lifestyle is of fundamental importance. Therefore, there is nothing to be ashamed of in being conscious of fashion. However, excess of everything is bad and should be avoided. Moderation should be the law in fashion as well. To live in style, dress well, colourfully and smartly makes life lively, attractive and zestful. In some mysterious way, it also gets linked to sex and its subtle and suggestive expression. Show and exhibitionism is part of a dynamic life and must be appreciated. Fashion-consciousness is a healthy sign as it appeals and pleases people, promotes togetherness, social interaction and enlivens the environment. It is misconceived to link fashion with immorality. But it would be certainly foolish to spend extravagantly on the latest fads and to run after them at the expense of valuable time, energy and resources. It is good to be fashionable but it is better to be simple and dignified because simplicity with dignity is the best and evergreen fashion. Change is the law of nature and so desirable and appreciable, but it does not mean slavish, blind and foolish aping and imitation of ideas, styles, manners and designs in dress, shoes, and hairstyles, etc. Our own folk, classical and standardised traditions, customs, manners are so rich, varied and unique that we can very well depend upon them to quench our thirst for change, novelty and innovation. ●

42. CHOOSING A CAREER

CASUAL approach in choosing a career or profession can prove very harmful. It reflects indecision, lack of dedication, purpose and carelessness. Gone are the days when birth, caste, heredity and family decided one's career. One followed the footsteps of one's father in India. Now, life is very complex and these are the days of specialisation. There is an infinite variety of professions and jobs, which may lead one

to confusion and bewilderment. It makes the choice of a career all the more difficult. The lack of proper guidance and counselling further worsens the situation. Consequently, young men and women are seen groping in the dark and making wrong career-choices. The ever-increasing number of job-seekers, ill-equipped to make right decisions in the matter, has generated a lot of frustration, hopelessness, alienation, unrest and acts of indiscipline. It also means a waste of human resources and national wealth.

The right and timely choice of a career is of fundamental importance. It is so crucial that the future success or failure of a person depends on it. A correct choice of career may lead to success, happiness and prosperity, while a wrong and late one may lead to sorrow, repentance, failure and lifelong frustration. The fruits of wrong and late decisions are numerous and bitter. To avoid these, one should try to choose one's career as early as possible, preferably at the high school stage, according to one's aptitude and resources. But school-going students are not the best judges in the matter as they are immature and inexperienced. They need sincere guidance, counselling and help, which can be very well provided by the teachers, counsellors, elders, and professional experts in the field.

Young people are ambitious and impatient. They aspire for top positions and careers without taking considering their skills, intellectual capacities, aptitudes, financial and other resources. A young man or woman may hitch his or her wagon to a top post or to the I.A.S. but may end up as a petty clerk or a receptionist. One may desire to become a star in the film-world and may end up as a mere casual artist or helper in the industry, or even worse. Choosing a profession for life is a little more than building castles in the air. It is no use shooting in the dark and hoping to hit the bull's eye. Vain efforts, ill-considered decisions and ill-conceived plans lead to repentance, failure, frustration and waste of national talent.

Our defective education and examination system and policies have further added to the confusion. What is needed now are immediate and fundamental changes in our education system, to vocationalise and diversify it at secondary level by introducing knowledge and skills that may enable a student to take up remunerative work without necessarily having to go in for higher education. There should be plenty of vocational courses to choose from at the +2 level. There should also be counselling and guidance services in each and every secondary school to help students in choosing their careers according to their aptitudes, skills, qualification and resources.

There are many training institutions, polytechnics, industrial training centres and professional colleges but they are not of much help in the absence of career guidance services. Therefore, the selection of the right profession and right institution has become difficult and complex and needs full consideration and professional approach. There are many careers and professions, such as teaching, engineering, law, technical trades, business, commerce, computer programming, banking, finance, journalism, publication, government employment, positions in police and armed forces, besides starting one's own shop, factory or workshop. Then, one can choose acting, films, commercial art, photography or become a stenographer. But each and every profession requires special skill, training and knowhow. One cannot choose a career at random.

Choosing a career is no more a matter of one's likes and dislikes. There are many other factors to be considered. Besides mental make up, capability and interest, the financial resources also have to be taken into account. One may want to become a doctor, executive, business entrepreneur or a computer engineer and may be well qualified to enter a medical, business or engineering college, but cannot do so if financial resources and the required means are lacking. In such a condition one will have to settle for some humble and less ambitious career. Change of career midstream may prove very risky, and so, a career should be selected very carefully and with full planning and deliberation and consultations with parents, teachers, elders, friends and professionals.

One can take to politics if one has an aptitude for public life and skills to make the people listen and follow. You need not pay heed to the saying that politics is the last refuge of the scoundrels. There have been many highly noble souls and personalities in politics. Take for example, Gandhiji, Pt. Nehru, Deshbandhu Chitranjan Das or Aruna Asaf Ali or Sarojini Naidu, to name only a few. It is a profession full of ups and downs, sudden reversals of fortunes and, at times, long drawn out struggle and strife. If you possess staunch optimism, strong determination, ambition for fame and popularity and are prepared to face the worst and yet turn it into the best, you are well-suited for the career of a politician. Similarly, if you are adventurous, bold and dashing, you can choose a military or a police career. There your abilities, skills, and aptitude, etc. will find full scope to flourish and blossom. If you have an aptitude for studies, books, magazines, learning and teaching, you may join the teaching profession as a teacher in a school or a lecturer in a college. Again, if you have enough money and resources and want to grow rich, you can choose to start your own business. The choice is yours but needs a very careful selection, for once you have chosen a career, it is not possible or advisable to retrace your steps. While choosing a career one stands at a cross-roads, with many roads converging on the point and you have to decide which one to take. Once the die is cast, there is no way out. In deciding your career you have to be practical, logical, rational, and shrewd. This is a crucial choice which will make or mar your future and also that of others who depend upon you. ●

43. SCIENTIFIC AND TECHNOLOGICAL DEVELOPMENT IN INDIA

THE modern age is the age of science, technology, knowledge and information. All these are the interrelated and different aspects of the same thing. Explosion of knowledge and information, based on breathtaking advancement in the field of science and technology, has bestowed on man powers enviable even for gods. It has helped man conquer space and time. Now he has unravelled many mysteries of nature and life and is ready to face new challenges and move forward in the realm of the unknown and the undiscovered.

In India there has been a long and distinct tradition of scientific research and technological advancement since ancient times. Since independence, we have accelerated our speed and efforts in this field and have established many research laboratories, institutions of higher learning and technical education. The results have been such as would make anybody's heart swell with pride, confidence and a sense of fulfilment. The best, however, is yet to come.

The central and state governments, various public and private sector establishments are engaged in scientific research and technological development to take the nation on the path of rapid development, growth and prosperity. There are about 200 research laboratories spread all over the country. The institutions of higher learning, and universities, the modern temples of learning, are all committed to take the country forward. They are well equipped and staffed to secure for the people of the nation all the blessings and benefits that can accrue from the acquisition and application of scientific knowledge and technology. But there is no room for complacency, for in this field only the sky is the limit and we are yet a developing country.

Our technology policy is comprehensive and well thought out. It aims at developing indigenous technology to ensure efficient absorption and adoption of imported technology suitable to national priorities and availability of resources. Its main objective is attainment of technical competence and self-reliance, leading to reduction in vulnerability in strategic and critical areas. With a view to strengthening our economy and industrial development, our government has introduced many structural reforms through adoption of a new industrial policy which has an important bearing on the programmes of development pertaining to science and technology. Consequently, technology has become our mainstay enterprise and now we have built a strong and reliable infrastructure for research, training and development in science and technology.

In the field of agriculture, our scientific and technological researches have enabled us to be self-reliant and self-sufficient in foodgrains. Today, we can withstand droughts and natural calamities with much greater confidence than ever before. Now, we are in a position to export foodgrains, etc. and are on the threshold of white and blue revolutions. Thanks to our agricultural scientists and farmers, always ready to imbibe new technologies, we have many varieties of hybrid seeds, crop-protection technologies, balanced farming practices and better water and irrigation management techniques. Similarly in the field of industrial research, we have achieved many milestones and India is emerging as a major industrial power of the world. The Council of Scientific and Industrial Research (CSIR), with its network of research laboratories and institutions, has been chiefly instrumental in our major achievements in scientific and industrial research. We have now joined the exclusive club of six advanced nations by developing our own super computer at the Centre for Development of Advance Computing (C-CAD) at Pune.

Our Atomic Research Commission, set up in 1948, is engaged in valuable nuclear research for peaceful purposes. The executive agency for implementing atomic energy programmes is the Department of Atomic Energy. The Bhabha Atomic Research Centre, Trombay, near Mumbai is the biggest single scientific establishment in the country, directing nuclear research. Now, we have five research reactors, including *Cirus*, *Dhruva*, *Zerina* and *Purnima*. We have carried out two underground nuclear tests at Pokharan in Rajasthan. This is a remarkable achievement by our nuclear scientists, which has enabled us to become one of the selected few countries of the world to have done it. India is also the first developing country, and one of the seven countries of the world to master fast breeding technology. Research in breeder technology is currently going on at Indira Gandhi Centre for Atomic Research at Kalpakkam, Chennai.

The successful launching of Polar Space Launching Vehicle (PSLV- D-2), in October 1994, marked India's entry into the league of the world's major space powers. In the INSAT-2 series of satellites, launched first in 1992, India has shown its ability to fabricate complex systems comparable to anything made anywhere in the world. Our previous launches of the SLV-3 and the SLV were merely stepping stones to what will be the workhorses of the business, the PSLV, which can launch one tonne satellite into orbit of up to 1000 km, and the

Geosynchronous Satellite Launch Vehicle, which can take 2.5 tonne satellite to orbits 36,000 km away. India's space programme rocketed to greater heights with the successful launch of the second Geosynchronous Satellite Launch Vehicle (GSLV-D2) in May, 2003. As has been rightly observed, the challenge before Indian Space Research Organisation (ISRO) is to maintain the momentum of the programme by integrating it with other missions. The most obvious ones are related to military communication and reconnaissance.

Our success on Antarctica speaks volumes of our scientific genius and technological wisdom in the field. So far, 13 scientific expeditions by our oceanographers, scientists and technicians have been to Antarctica and we have two permanent stations on the icy continent.

In the field of defence also our achievements have been quite laudable. The successful production of such missiles as *Prithvi* and *Nag* testify to the high capabilities and achievements of our scientists. We have also been successful in producing opto-electronic fire control and night-vision devices required for our indigenous tanks. The HAL at Bangalore has already produced Advanced Light Helicopter (ALH).

Obviously, technology has been used effectively as a tool and instrument of national development and yet much remains to be achieved in order to make its benefits reach the masses. Scientists in the country will have to strive hard to take technological developments to people's doorsteps. Therefore, they cannot rest on their laurels, but should remember the famous and inspiring lines of the poet Robert Frost :

The woods are lovely, dark and deep,
But I have promises to keep,
And miles to go before I sleep,
And miles to go before I sleep. ●

44. FOREIGN POLICY OF INDIA

INDIA'S foreign policy is based on the principles of non-alignment and Panchsheela. India firmly believes in peaceful co-existence, self-reliance, co-operation non-alignment, support for decolonisation disarmament, removal of inequalities among the nations and global struggle against apartheid and racialism. The basic objective of the policy is to preserve India's freedom of options and decision-making in a world full of rivalry among powerful nations for supremacy and dominance.

Having undergone some of the worst experiences of foreign rule and imperialism, India has always supported the cause of freedom and struggle against discrimination, whether racial, economic or political. India extended its full support to Indonesia in its struggle for independence. In the 1950s, during the Korean crisis, India bluntly refused to take sides and remained neutral while calling for a peaceful solution. Similarly, in 1956, when the Suez Canal crisis threatened world-peace in the wake of British-French-Israel aggression on Egypt, India played a constructive role by condemning the attack and urged its immediate termination. India's contribution to maintain peace and avoid conflicts can also be seen in its full support to the U.N. in its peacekeeping measures. Indian diplomats and military personnel have been participating in the world body's peacekeeping operations in various troubled parts of the world like Congo, Lebanon, Cyprus, Yugoslavia, Cambodia, and Somalia, etc.

India has also been instrumental in transforming the British Commonwealth into the present Commonwealth. Among the member countries, India always pleaded the case of South African people and played a key role for rallying opinion against apartheid and the minority white regime, which has since been voted out of power. Similarly, India's role as a leading member of the Non-Aligned Movement (NAM) has been very positive and constructive on major international issues. Through this organisation, India has always supported acceleration of the struggle against colonialism, economic of and domination, discrimination against the poor and developing countries by the developed and rich countries. During the tenth NAM summit held in September 1992 at Jakarta, India urged the member countries to give the highest priority to such issues as nuclear disarmament, elimination of the last vestiges of colonialism, eradication of poverty and accelerated economical development of the South-based countries.

India has welcomed the end of the so-called Cold War in the wake of the *detente* between the two superpowers. At the same time, however, it is aware that their contribution to global disarmament is almost nil and has, therefore, refused to sign the Nuclear Non-Proliferation Treaty (NPT). India has opposed the NPT because it is discriminatory and against the interests of developing countries.

India wants the superpowers of the world to not only stop producing nuclear weapons but to also destroy the existing ones. Further, China should also be brought to the negotiating table and there should be significant reduction in the defence budgets of the five permanent members of the Security Council. India is against discrimination in any form. India also insists that, instead of bilateral negotiations, all disarmament negotiations should be held under the auspices of the U.N. to make them transparent, fair, universal and non-discriminatory.

India's prestige has been ever on the increase because of its independent foreign policy based on non-alignment. India believes in settlement of all the issues by peaceful means, across the table and through talks and negotiations. India wants to maintain peaceful and friendly relations with Pakistan and settle all major issues, including that of Kashmir, through talks and negotiations according to the Shimla Agreement. India wants peaceful and friendly relations with Pakistan in spite of the latter's belligerent mood, aggressive postures and support to terrorist activities in Jammu and Kashmir. India firmly believes in co-operation, the principle of 'live and let live', and normalisation of relations among all the nations of the world.

India wants to nuclear energy to be used for peaceful purposes only. And, it has been practicing what it has been preaching. India also supports the non-proliferation treaty, provided it is not biased and partisan. India has made special efforts to improve its relations with neighbouring countries. Consequently, today India's relations with China, Sri Lanka, and Nepal, etc., have been very cordial, healthy and purposeful. There has been an exchange of many visits and several treaties and pacts for economic development, industrial growth and cultural exchanges have been signed. By and large, India's foreign policy has been successful in protecting its image as a peace-loving, non-aligned country, an emerging power, dedicated to world peace and prosperity. ●

45. SUPERSTITIONS

SUPERSTITIONS betray human weakness, ignorance and fear of the unknown and mysterious. They are the irrational belief in things which remain inexplicable, mysterious and unravelled because of lack of sufficient knowledge and scientific temper. Superstitions are on the decline because of spread of education, reasoning and scientific advancement. However, even educated and advanced people have their superstitions. It has also been seen that while many old superstitions are dying, new ones are being born. Primitive instincts, fears and beliefs present a fertile land for superstitions. Emotional instability, religious orthodoxy, blind belief in irrational rituals, customs and practices make people an easy prey of the superstitions.

Superstitions are not confined to a particular part of the globe, people, race or community. They are ubiquitous and found throughout the world, in one form or another. There is only a difference of degrees. They are more prevalent among illiterate, uneducated and scientifically less advanced people and societies. Superstitions are being passed on from one generation to another, through religious practices. No doubt they are gradually losing ground with the advancement of rationality, scientific approach to things and globalisation of the world, yet, superstitions may not be eradicated for a long time.

Belief in charms, supernatural powers, ghosts, evil spirits, and spiritual healing, etc., have their deep roots in superstitions. They are common among the people of all classe. For example, the eclipse of the sun and moon, sighting of shooting stars and comets, cries of certain birds like owls, ravens, and wailing of dogs, mewing of cats, howling of jackals and braying of the ass at certain hours are still regarded as ominous in many communities all over the world. The fear of number 13 is another example of our blind belief. All superstitions have their origin in the human psychology of fear of ill-luck, insecurity and the dread of inexplicable forces in nature. When some phenomena cannot be explained and understood, people start fearing them and assign them divine, supernatural and mysterious origins.

In ancient days, all races and people were governed by superstitions. They found rich and fertile ground in human ignorance and lack of scientific knowledge. The less a community is educated and enlightened, the more it tends to be superstitious and backward. Some vested interests, like the priestly class etc., also exercise a great influence in spreading, maintaining and generating new superstitions. Many of our religious, sectarian and family rituals and rites are based on blind beliefs, and tricks are being played on gullible people by the so-called godmen, priests, quacks, charlatans, astrologers, palmists, star and crystal gazers. There are many religious cults thriving today throughout the world only because of human ignorance, blind faith and irrationality. Even the developed countries are no exception. In spite of advancement of science and technology, the hold of superstitions on mankind is strong and man continues to suffer from these evils and complexes born out of them. In India, sneezing when someone is about to start work, is considered inauspicious. Similarly, the crossing of the path by a cat, especially a black one, is regarded as boding ill-luck. Like these ominous signs, there are lucky ones as well, which are regarded as harbingers of good luck, fortune and success. Man's ingrained fear of the unknown and the inexplicable has invented ominous signs, portents and premonitions.

Sacrifice of birds and animals to please the gods and goddesses, and to atone for one's sins, is a common practice among many communities all over the world. Many women are still lynched because they are mistaken for witches. People still resort to magicians and godmen to exorcise the so-called evil spirits and their harmful influences, and are being willingly fleeced and duped in the process.

Superstitions are thriving in an organised way under various cults, religious sects, godmen, priests, and so-called prophets and representatives of gods. They are successfully leading the masses by the nose. We have actually failed to draw a line between religion and blind faith, bigotry and spiritualism and between prayer and useless incantations. We regard certain hours and days as inauspicious and so consult astrologers, priests and godmen to know the auspicious days and hours to start our work, projects and journey. Likewise, the time and date of marriage, inauguration, foundation-laying ceremonies are fixed according to the advice of astrologers and the positions of the planets and stars.

The need of the hour is to cultivate more and more objectivity, rationality and scientific spirit in our approach to things, including those which are inexplicable and in some way or other mysterious. We need not give up our ideals, imagination, emotions and impulses and become living robots, but we must be alert and watchful so as not to allow these to dominate and dictate our faculties of reasoning, logic and analysis. Religion is certainly blind if not blended with science and reasoning; and, science is lame, unless guided by conscience and emotions. Our only hope is in sanity, balance and cultivation of scientific outlook and temper. ●

46. NOISE POLLUTION

THE rapid degradation of environment is the result of our over indulgence. This can be seen in the poisoned air, polluted water, mountains of garbage and waste, deafening noise and smoke-belching vehicles all around. Much of the wholesomeness of the environment has been destroyed during the past few decades, resulting in dangerous imbalance in nature and ecology. Our current concern about environment and its increasing pollution, though belated, is welcome.

Pollution has many dimensions and faces, and noise pollution is one of them. But public awareness about the dangers of noise pollution is still insufficient and, therefore, nothing substantial has been done against it. The knowledge among people about noise as a dangerous pollutant is miserably low and poor.

It is really sad that very few people are aware of the fact that noise is a great pollutant. It is all around us. There is traffic noise, household noise, construction and industrial noise, loud music, noise coming from religious places through loudspeakers, noise of marriage, religious and political processions, rallies, and in the sky there is noise of the aeroplanes and helicopters. Yet, we remain unaware of its harmful presence and effects. This dangerous pollutant disturbs our sleep and peace, causes irritation and annoyance, interrupts our flow of thoughts and affects our mental and physical health.

It is as dangerous and widespread as the atmospheric or water pollution. Studies have proved that constant exposure to loud noise results in many mental disorders and physical ailments. Our sensitive ears cannot shut out noise, neither when we are awake nor asleep. So there is a continuous onslaught on our ears in cities, towns and places where industries are located. It is because of this pollution that we have lost much of our sensitivity to finer, softer and subtler sounds.

The relative loudness of a sound is measured in decibels. The lowest audible sound is one decibel. Sounds up to approximately 70 decibels are tolerable but louder sounds become harmful in proportion to their upward increase on the scale. Decibel levels of 90 are a threat to ears and beyond that may cause permanent deafness to a person exposed to it for long periods.

The ubiquity of loud and constant noise produced by traffic, machines, hi-fi music systems, factories, public address systems, aeroplanes, and railway engines, etc. in towns and cities has made life very uncomfortable and intolerable. Consequently, people living in cities and towns do not know what is real peace, proper rest and deep sleep. Even during night there is great noise emanating from factories, sirens, trains and their engines and zooming aeroplanes in the skies. This noise may not arouse us from our sleep but it certainly affects us adversely in many ways. It affects our working, both in terms of quality and quantity.

Noise may sometimes go unnoticed but it certainly produces profound psychological changes in the body and mind.

Frequent exposure to loud noise causes decreased flow of blood in the small vessels, dilation of pupils, tensing of muscles, digestive problems, nervousness, irritation and anxiety. It also lowers the working efficiency, especially in jobs requiring concentration, accuracy and speed. The most glaring effect of noise can be seen in the form of gradual loss of hearing, resulting in deafness.

With the passage of time and increased industrial activity and urbanisation, noise is becoming all pervasive and distracting. Even villages are now no more immune from this nuisance and pollutant.

We are now living virtually in a babel of noises and leading a life sans sanity, sans peace and mental equipoise. Many of our quarrels, acts of irrationality, traffic accidents, and crimes, etc. are the direct result of this kind of living.

City dwellers are in great danger of gradually becoming hard of hearing and ultimately deaf, if it is not noticed and cured in time. The conclusion: more public awareness about the dangers of this pollutant and stricter implementation of the noise control laws. Only increased public awareness can properly deal with the menace, which is growing louder and more dangerous every day. A new concept suggests that planting of trees can also reduce the menace to some extent. Then why not to go green as much and as fast as possible?

●

47. SCIENCE IN THE SERVICE OF MAN

SCIENCE has opened and enlarged new frontiers of human knowledge, information, achievement, comforts and conveniences. Now we have a window, large enough to peep into the hitherto unknown, dark and mysterious areas of nature in the form of modern science. This passage from ignorance to knowledge, from darkness to light, from superstitions and blind beliefs to scientific temper and rationality, has been a long struggle, full of strife, labour, sweat and challenges. But

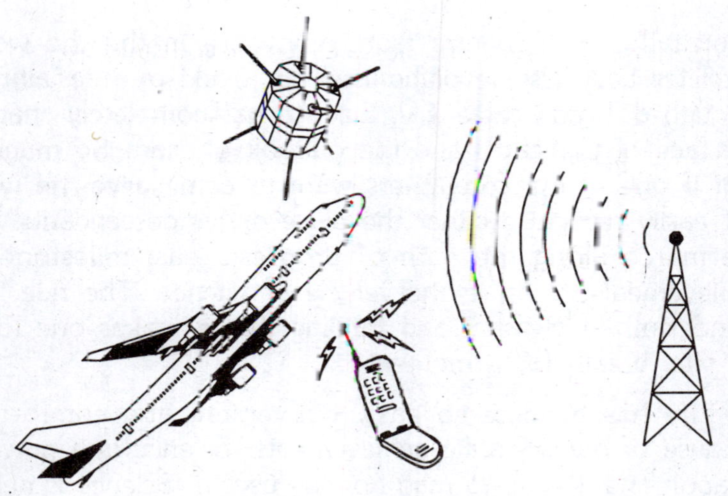

it is man's nature to seek and face challenges and his destiny to overcome them.

Man's endless thirst for knowledge and conquest has resulted in phenomenal advancement of science in each and every walk of life and so the modern age has rightly been christened as the Age of Science. Science means reasoning, analysis, objectivity and systematic study of things. Science is very comprehensive, universal, all-inclusive, simple and yet very complex and so beyond the approach of a satisfying definition. It may not be defined but touches all of us at all the places and times. Its expression is universal, unambiguous and palpable and well understood by the educated people in most of the cases. People know that science has helped man to conquer time and space and the world has turned into a global village. Now, the moon is in the palm of his hand and planets are not too far off for his scrutiny and study. We have supersonic planes and will soon have hypersonic planes to enable us cover the distance between Tokyo and New York in just 2 hours. Satellite communication has ushered in instantaneous contact from one corner of the globe to another. Instant communication through cordless, cellular and mobile telephones, paging, and electronic mail, etc. are really wonderful. Then there are computers, which help retrieve any information you require from anywhere in the the world. Satellites have also revolutionised our world of entertainment through dish and cable T.V. Science has completely changed the face of the earth and the outlook of man. So much so that if one of our forefathers were to come alive, he would not easily recognise either the place or his descendants. And the march along the path of progress, past milestones of achievements, is on in the vehicle of science. The ride is so wonderful, so pleasant and thrilling that it makes one forget his vital breath for a moment.

Life has become so easy, convenient and comfortable because of our scientific achievements. Science is a powerful weapon and it is up to man how he uses it. Science is neither a blessing nor a curse in itself. It is knowledge—pure, powerful, universal and absorbing—always at our service, command and bidding. Its aim is to serve sincerely but it is our prerogative to decide what service we ask science to render. Therefore, it is unwise to categorise science as evil or good.

Science has helped us in eradicating many diseases, which were fatal in the past, and in treating many others. Now transplantation of many vital organs is a common medical practice. As a result of many medical discoveries and inventions, man finds himself more safe, secure and his age lengthened. It is because of many scientific teachings and learning-aids that distant education is so popular, cheap and universal. Science has turned learning into a pleasure.

The wonders and achievements of science are too many. Take for example, the harnessing of nuclear energy. It has broadened the horizons of power to be used to run mills, factories, engines, railways, to light up homes and streets, to energise pumpsets and tubewells, to smoothen earth-moving and mining work, to be used in irradiation, to preserve seafood and other food items and sterilisation of medicines, to name only a few of the areas. There are many other areas which have immensely benefited by it. It is a great and inexhaustible power with huge potentialities.

Again, the world of scientific appliances is no less wonderful. Now man has more time because of these gadgets and conveniences. Science has helped man to leapfrog into a new, bold and wonderful world of fantastic achievements, comforts and conveniences. No doubt, the other side of the coin shows the darker visage of science. The misuse of science and its inventions has brought the entire humanity on the brink of destruction and annihilation. It has produced very dangerous weapons, like nuclear bombs, missiles, and fatal and poisonous nerve gases, etc., but again it needs to be underlined that science is neither good nor bad. It is knowledge, it is power, a boon and gift, a key to unlock the secrets of nature. If we misuse it, we are to blame. ●

48. HOW TO ACHIEVE SUCCESS

HOW to achieve success? What is the secret of success? Why are a few so lucky as to possess it while many others fail? Why does nothing succeed like success? These are some of the important questions which often trouble us. These also clearly show how important success is. Ask the people who have no taste of it. According to Emily Dickenson, "Success is counted sweetest by those who never succeed. To comprehend a nectar/Requires sorest need." No doubt most of the people are in dire need of it for they have never tasted its nectar. Even those who have its taste would consider themselves most unfortunate when deprived of it. The history of mankind shows that only those who have been spectacularly successful in their attempts find place in it.

The path to success lies through struggle, strife, hard work, sweat and sometimes even blood. To achieve success is not easy and to maintain it, even more difficult.

Hard labour ultimately wins. Therefore, it is necessary that people who desire to be successful, give in to hard labour and work. The same thought is expressed by R.L. Stevenson thus : "To travel hopefully is better than to arrive, and the true success is to labour."

For success one needs 99% perspiration and only 1% inspiration. There is no substitute for hard work. Perseverance and sweat alone takes one to the top. Those who talk of luck, intelligence and intuition as the only steps of the ladder leading to success, are not to be believed. Nothing great, good and lasting can be achieved by inspiration or insight alone. Patience, perseverance, perspiration, and labour, etc., form the rock-foundation on which you can build your mansion of success. Even with great luck and genius, people have had to toil hard to be successful and famous as politicians, actors, painters, musicians, businessmen, sportspersons or men of letters. Perseverance and perspiration are the other names of good fortune and success. Most of the people fail only because their efforts are feeble, half-hearted and they lack the quality of a good and hardworking animal. Remember the story of King Bruce? He could succeed and vanquish his enemy because he never lost courage and heart, made persistent efforts until finally he had success and the spider showed the way. Tenzing Norgay, only a sherpa and porter, became world famous for his conquest of the Mount Everest but he had to make more than a dozen attempts before success and victory finally came.

It is said rightly that where there is a will there is a way. Strong determination, will power and motivation are the other necessary ingredients of success. The word "impossible" is only in the dictionary of fools and the frail. Nothing is impossible or unachievable in the world, if the efforts are in the right direction and backed by a strong will. Our desires mostly remain unfulfilled because they are mere wishes. They lack strong urge and motivation. God helps those who help themselves. We should differentiate between "will" and a wish. Will means unfliching determination, perseverance, labour and struggle, leading to sweet success and fulfilment. Will power is a great motivating force, more powerful than atomic energy. It has changed the course of history and fortunes of mankind. Remember Alexander, Chanakya, Joan of Arc, Tilak and Napoleon. They were the very embodiments of strong will power. The same common clay of determination was used in shaping them out.

Nothing can defeat one's purpose if it is backed by strong resolve and determination, not even heavy odds, abject poverty and hardships. A determined person can even snatch victory and success from the jaws of defeat. Such a man can win great battles against heavy odds and large armies with a handful of determined and dedicated soldiers. There is no gain without pain. Such a person does not believe in luck or favours of Dame Fortune. His faith is always in himself, and his determination is always firm as a rock, and so, ultimately, he is bound to be crowned with success.

Another important requirement of success is doing things then and there. Procrastination is a thief of time. Know the value of time. Time is precious, more valuable than money and riches. Lost time can never be recovered or compensated. Time is opportunity; once lost, it never returns. All successful men and women, and all great persons have been great economisers of time. They have always been punctual in their habits and work. Culture and civilisation, great discoveries and inventions, conquests and achievements owe much to them who have made the best use of time and opportunities. They never waited for an opportunity but created one for themselves. They did the maximum in minimum time. For them, life was too short and there was so much to be done and achieved. A proper use of time means proper use of opportunity. Remember the famous words of Shakespeare, if you want to achieve success :

There is a tide in the affairs of man.
Which, taken at the flood, leads on to fortune;
Omitted, all the voyage of their life
Is bound in shallows and miseries.
On such a full sea are we are afloat
And we must take the current when it serves
Or lose our ventures.

Always define your aims objectives and priorities well with care and then pursue them honestly, with your full heart, mind and soul. Having decided your aim, move forward with steady steps towards it, without looking left or right. Remember Arjuna and his shooting of the clay-bird on the tree under the tutelage of his guru Dronacharya. Never be ashamed of your work and position, however humble it might be. Cherish it with all your being because all work is sacred, so perform it well. Even if you are engaged in shoe-making, make your shoes perfect. This is the only secret of success. Be always a learner. Learn from others and from objects of nature. Know your strengths and weaknesses and enlarge the former and reduce and finally eliminate the latter. Never find fault with your luck or tools; always engage yourself in doing the right thing, in the right place and time to achieve success. Never forget that good aims are not sufficient, they must be achieved by noble means. Aims are significant but so are the means. Success is also a means and never an end in itself. ●

49. WHY DO I PLAY CHESS?

I PLAY chess in my free time because it is my hobby and passion. There are a number of hobbies to choose from but I find chess the best and most fascinating. For me there cannot be a better pursuit than playing chess in my spare time. It not only keeps me busy but also gives entertainment, provides a welcome change and creative satisfaction. However, it is never an obsession with me. It best suits my aptitude and liking.

I was initiated into the game by my late father when I was just 6 years old. My father was a very good player of chess and would play it on Sundays and other holidays in the afternoon with his friend. It was really fascinating to see them get so absorbed in it that it made them forget everything around them. Their playing sessions would sometimes extend into late nights. Sometimes, when there was a power-failure or load-shedding, they would continue their game in candlelight. I learnt the finer points and strategies of the game by watching them play.

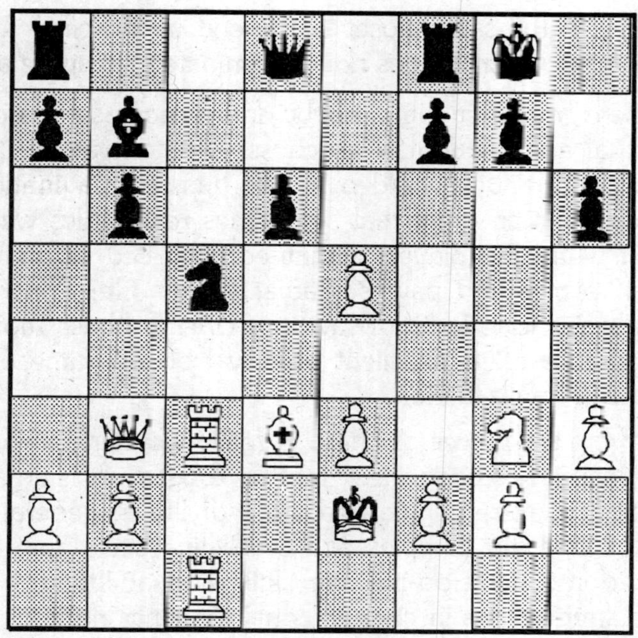

Thus, it is perhaps in my blood. It is quite an intellectual game and diversion and also an art that creates beauty and lasting pleasure. There is no other game or human diversion that reflects so well the vast range of encounters and situations of life as does chess. It reminds me of the famous *Rubaiyat* of Omar Khayyam, the prince of the wise, who in a poignant mood exclaimed :

But helpless pieces of the game He plays
Upon the chequered board of nights and days;
Hither and thither moves, and checks and slays,
And one by one back in the closet lays.

For Shakespeare, all the world was a stage and all the persons actors. For Omar Khayyam the world is a mere chessboard, the people chessmen, and God, the creator, the player. Do we not begin our life like chessman, equal in the closet, place the board of life to play our difficult roles as Pawns, Knights, Bishops, Rooks, Queens and Kings? Do we not become equal again in the sight of our Creator, as he returns us to the same closet at the end of the play? Death is the greatest leveller. It does not discriminate or it spare anyone.

Is there any other game, hobby or diversion as philosophical, intellectual and thoughtful as chess? No, not at all. It is an ageless game and its hold over the human imagination and mind has been so great that sometimes real battles were won and lost while the players remained absorbed in their mock battle of pieces and pawns. Satyajit Ray's film *Shatranj Ke Khilari*, was the only film I saw in a cinema house more than once, because of its excellent portrayal of the game of chess in such a trying situation.

The captive power of chess is really wonderful. For many a great man it has been their "mother tongue". It is an abstract expression of the struggle and strife of life in general and is useful for studying complex and conflicting situations. It helps in developing decision-making skills and abilities. A chess-player's strength lies in clear, rational thinking, right approach, logic, knowledge and ability not to commit a mistake. His power of vision, vigilance, intuition and imagination are what make him stronger than others. A game of chess means leisure time spent creatively and purposefully. It activates the central nervous system and develops positive emotional reaction. It is good training for those engaged in challenging tasks and intellectual pursuits. A player of chess is required to make a decisive move in a very complex situation and that too under pressure of time and that is what is required from people in many challenging professions.

Chess players have been found to possess a higher spatial ability than others of comparable intelligence levels. They also possess greater physical endurance, together with tolerance of frustration. A game of chess is a manifestation of both the will to win and create beauty, with the player aiming to surmount all complexity, rigours and barriers to realise his plan and ideas. It appeals to me most because it involves, at every move, at each stage, intensiveness, enterprise, resourcefulness, self-control, determination, vision and the quick execution of the plan.

It is an epic game, with the chessboard being like a battlefield and the two sets of pieces the two contending armies, and the two rival players think in terms of attack, defence, capture, threats, manoeuvres, ambushes and tactics. The game is full of such activities which suggest a real and live combat. It is a game purely of Indian origin; a great tribute to Indian genius. In ancient India, it was known as *Chaturanga*, which means the four limbs or diversions of ancient Indian army: infantry, cavalry, elephants and chariots. Those four divisions or limbs formed the army proper, flanking on either side of the king and his chief minister or mantri/vazir. ●

50. DANCES OF INDIA

MAN'S spiritual urge and inner drive manifested in rhythmic body movement constitute an art form called dance. Thus, rhythm and movements are basic to dance, creation and existence. Men, birds, beasts, plants, and the earth, all are engaged in a ceaseless cosmic dance-recital. Rhythm and movement is life, and its cessation stagnation, decay and death. Dance symbolises both evolution and involution. Recent researches have revealed that distant galaxies are dancing away from us at an immense speed, some of them at the rate of about 144,000 km per second. Man is destined to dance his way to higher levels of consciousness and evolution till he achieves fullness, fulfilment and perfection.

It is in this background that Indian dances can be best appreciated and understood. The aesthetic foundations of the Indian dances and other art-forms are laid on the rocks of spiritual sadhana and rigorous mental and physical discipline leading to liberation, however, fleeting and momentary in the beginning. In essence, Indian dances are deeply religious in their origin. They do not simply involve legs and limbs, but the whole body and soul.

Indian classical dances are highly developed and stylised and have changed little in their technique, and yet they are innovative. By and large, they strictly adhere to the principles and rules laid down by Bharat Muni in his *Natyashastra* many ages ago. They, along with no less fascinating and variegated folk-forms, present a panoramic and spectacular view of splendid and continuous dance tradition of the country. Their history, spanning from the prehistoric times to the present, makes a fascinating study and reading. Indian dances, particularly the classical dances, are famous all over the world. There are said to be 180 styles of Indian dancing, and 101 of these are described in the *Natyashastra*. Most of these dance-styles can be seen depicted on the walls and pillars of some of the famous Indian temples. Music, dance and drama have been integral parts of Indian religion and life.

Of the classical dances, the five very famous ones are :

(i) Bharat Natyam
(ii) Kathakali
(iii) Manipuri
(iv) Kathak
(v) Odissi

Bharat Natyam is popular in south India. Feeling, raga and rhythm play a most crucial role in this dance form. It is the oldest dance-form and is associated with Lord Shiva. It is a solo dance, and most complicated and subtle to be understood and appreciated by a layman. Preserved in its prestine glory and unalloyed purity in Tamil Nadu, it enjoys very wide currency and popularity in India. For centuries in medieval India, it was performed by Devadasis or handmaids of gods in the exquisite temples of south India. The Devadasis were then held in high esteem as repositories of culture and performing arts.

Bharat Natyam's three components—movement, mime and music—contribute equally in performance and recital. It is also a tender and erotic dance, generally performed by a female dancer and sometimes by a male dancer as well. No doubt it is based on the theme of love, romance and heroism but it is invariably devotional in essence and never sensual. It is equally and evenly divided into *nritta* (abstract dance) and *nritya* (expressive dance). It is presented in such a way that it upholds itself in a sequence of stages like a bud bursting into a blossom of unmatched beauty, colour, fascination and splendour. The artist performing Bharat Natyam wears a costume which is both traditional as well as functional. A wide variety of beautiful ornaments are also used.

Kathakali, the traditional story-play of kaleidoscopic Kerala, was evolved and nurtured in temples, just like Bharat Natyam. It is also known as *Attakatha* (dance-play) and is fundamentally of epic dimensions. Its journey from temples to courts and then to streets, courtyards and public places in Kerala tells its ever-increasing universal appeal and popularity. Kathakali is performed in open air, on a square stage with a tall and massive brass lamp, fed with coconut oil, set in front of the dancers at the centre of the stage. This is the only lighting used. The continuous thundering of the drum called *chenda* heralds the performance of the Kathakali dance-drama. The theme to be enacted and danced may either be from the *Ramayana*, the *Mahabharata*, the *Puranas*, or the *Vedas*. It continues all through the night, to the accompaniment of singing, drumming and playing on the large bronze cymbals. Traditionally, young boys perform female roles, but now girls and women also perform female roles. The prospective

Kathakali dancers are caught young and initiated ritually in the art at the tender age of 10–12 and made to undergo a rigorous and intensive training and discipline under a skilled guru or master. The costumes are traditional, gorgeous, spectacular, varied, ostentatious, ornamental and yet functional. Eyes play an exceptional role in this style of dance.

Manipuri dances are based on the romance of divine Krishna and Radha. It was Maharaja Jai Singh, also known as Bhagy Chandra, who helped to develop and patronise this dance form. His daughter Princess Bimba-manjari was a dancer par excellence of this style. It was subsequently formalised, codified and stylised on classical lines by great gurus of the art. The Rasa-dances are always related to Krishna legends and the movements of the neck, the breasts and hips are not allowed in this dance as they are considered vulgar and below the dignity and grandeur of these devotional forms of dance. The text of the accompanying songs is always from great saint-poets like Jayadeva, Vidyapati, Chandidas or from the *Bhagvat Purana*. The costume is always rich, ornamental and captivating. Rich in emotional content and sentiment of love, Manipuri dances require arduous training and discipline of the artist from a very tender age under the guidance of expert gurus. Truly classical, devotional and religious in spirit, these are perfomed to the singing of songs and *kirtans* and to the accompaniment of *khol, mridanga, manjira* and bamboo flutes. Their liquid beauty, lyrical quality, restrained and rhythmic swaying, swinging and spinning, with hands close to the body, coupled with soft music, lend the performance a uniqueness and divinity which defy description.

Kathak, a major classical dance form of north India, is performed both by men and women. It is well-known for its spontaneity, freedom from uniformity, and has a lot of room for innovation and improvisation. It enjoys a fair amount of individuality and autonomy. A kathak dancer can change his or her sequence of stages to suit individual style and aptitude. Kathak makes a great use of a number of Hindustani musical compositions like Dhrupad, Hori, Dhamal, Pad, Bhajan,

Thumri, Ghazal, and Dadra, etc. It may also begin with an invocation of gods. There is a rich variety in repertoire as far as expression of feelings and passions are concerned. In an expressional dance, the artist combines mime with music and dance and interprets the song to the accompaniment of soft music of the *sarangi* or a *sitar*. The songs, either in Hindi, Braj or Hindustani, may be sacred, secular, devotional or erotic.

Odissi, the classical dance form of Orissa is highly inspired, impassioned, ecstatic and sensuous. In medieval days, this dance was performed by the Devadasis, called Maharis, in the temples. Rooted deeply in traditions and rituals, the dance is very old though its name is new. It commences with an invocation of gods to the accompaniment of rhythmic vocal syllables blended into drum-beats. The chant of the musician, the beat of the drum and the lilting and measured foot movements of the danseuse are so harmonised as to produce a delicate balance between the danseuse and the dance. The audience is ushered into a fascinating world of mime, music and motifs, reflecting sculpture stances. It represents a fine synthesis of *Lasya* and *Tandava* styles of Indian classical dances. It has an idiom that transcends all the limits of communication, leading to a rich, aesthetic and spiritual experience.

Indian folk dances have relatively far greater free play, expression of feelings, emotions and sentiments than classical forms. The folk people are born dancers. Their gait, movements and various activities, specially those of women, betray their rhythmic tempo and sculpturesque poses and postures. Folk dance-forms are intimately connected with the performer's life, daily activities, environment and other physical surroundings and nature in its various moods and season. Indian folk dances are ever fresh, fragrant and imbued with a wonderful capacity to renew and to imbibe new influences and yet to maintain tradition and continuity. Indian folk dances are part and parcel of the country's rich cultural heritage and immense artistic wealth. Their staggering variety and richness inspires wonder and admiration. They are at once thoroughly religious, social, ceremonial, seasonal, material, ritual, romantic and erotic and always inspired by mythology, legends, scriptures, folk tales and, above all, by the most primitive instinct to express pain and pleasure through linear and statuesque stances and rhythmic movements. ●

51. SELF-RELIANCE

SELF-RELIANCE or self-help is a must to achieve success, happiness and progress. It is of no use to wait for others to help, assist and guide. The saying, "God helps those who help themselves," very beautifully and aptly underlines the truth. Only the weak and helpless call on gods for help instead of putting their own shoulders to the wheel. One must learn to trust one's own hands, power and strength instead of depending on good luck and the grace of the gods. Man is his own friend or foe. It is he himself who can make or mar his fortune. One is what one chooses to be. Lord Buddha taught man to be one's own lamp and light and not to depend on borrowed light. Shelley, the great English poet, once remarked that God has given man arms long enough to reach the skies, if he should only put them out.

A self-reliant person depends on his own brain, power, capacity, resources, and prudence. Therefore, he is master of his fate and fortune. He shapes his own course of events and is never a slave of circumstances. Equipoise, confidence, alertness, perseverance and patience are his sure tools with which he carves out success and happiness. Such a person is firm, prompt in action, decisive, bold, self-possessed and ever ready to face any challenge anytime, while others are much handicapped and doubtful starters. They lack self-confidence, independence of judgement and action. Success is the sweetest when earned with one's own sweat, labour, perseverance and resources. Fruits of success wouldn't taste as sweet if achieved with the help of others. One can never run fast with crutches. Dependence on others is like working with crutches. The lesson of self-reliance is one that all young men and women should learn and imbibe if they want to succeed in life. It never means that he or she should not take into consideration the advice and counsel of their friends, well-wishers and elders. Self-help also never means not learning from the experiences of others. It only means that one should not depend on these nor should they be ever expected. One may accept co-operation, and guidance, etc. when willingly offered but, "God helps those who helps themselves" should always be their guiding principle and light.

It is with determination and self-reliance that all hurdles can be removed one by one. There is no substitute for hard work and toil. Therefore, never hesitate to soil your hands, to shed your sweat and to depend on your strength.

Be your own guide, lamp, staff and help and never crave for favour if you desire to achieve a respectable measure of success. Heaven and hell, victory and defeat lie within you. It is up to you what you choose. You are the maker and master of your destiny. Never think it is decided and governed by any force outside you. Self-reliant people are always optimistic, cheerful, positive thinkers, decisive, free, independent, reliable, courageous and people of character and destiny. They are rich in expediency, quick action and steadfast in resolve. They never blame fate, circumstances, or lack of opportunities because they can create opportunities and make their own tools and use them with all the skill, strength, precision and concentration at their command. Their work, creation, achievement, and success all bear the stamp of their personality, character and authority. They are the real heroes and the chosen ones. They are original in ideas and imagination in shaping things and events. They achieve what they do because they are self-reliant, resolute, single-minded and-self-disciplined. They know their strengths and weaknesses and use their power, energies, resources, skills and capabilities in such a way as to never to show a chink in their armour.

All great and successful people have been self-reliant. They led their people and achieved what they had set their minds on. For example, take the case of countries depending on foreign aid. These countries are always slaves and in a debt-trap. They cannot take independent decisions and shape their foreign policies without taking into consideration the interests of their debtor-masters. They receive economic aid but there are always strings attached to it.

It is your own industry, wisdom and perseverance that can take you to the top. Many times, it has been found that help or overhelp actually spoiled the career of many a promising young man and woman. Spoon-feeding is undesirable. It is said of Michaelangelo that he devoted 16 hours every day to the study and practice of his art. He often rose at midnight to continue the labour of the day, and the light by which he worked and handled his tools, came from a bit of a candle fixed to the top of his cap of paste-board.

Gandhiji has been a great and living example of self-reliance and self-help. He always depended on his own inner strength, moral power and character. It was because of his unmatched power of self-reliance that he could lead such a huge nation like India and defeat such a powerful adversary as the Britishers, and that too without any bloodshed, violence or armed struggle. Though so frail in body, his self-confidence, born-out of his spirit of self-reliance, was unique and wonderful. The strength of his moral character, self-reliance and self-dependence has few parallels in human history. Napoleon said that the word 'impossible' was found in the dictionary of fools. And he was right. A self-reliant person is always wise, practical and sure, nothing is impossible for him. There is no substitute for self-reliance; no external help can replace it.

Beggars cannot be choosers. But a self-reliant person's selection, decision and determination always prevail; he is a chooser and selector for he is not a beggar. Self-reliance brings out the best in men and women, while dependence on others weakens our will power, resolve, judgement and striking power. The odds and unfavourable circumstances work like a healthy challenge and inspiration to a self-reliant person. Sufferings refine our sensibilities; sweet are the uses of adversity, and struggle and strife make us strong and tolerant. Self-reliance and power to overcome odds are two aspects of the same coin. Unfavourable circumstances, odds, and difficulties, etc., test our courage, strength, character and self-reliance. The path of self-reliance is strewn with thorns, stones and traps but at the end there are flowers of success, glory, prosperity and fame. Let us not lose heart when beset by difficulties, or oppressed with failure, for these things are designed to stimulate us to higher and purer effort, and to teach us the great and glorious lesson of self-reliance. Undoubtedly, self-reliance is a pilgrim's best staff, a worker's best tool, and a soldier's best weapon. Therefore, be a self-helper. ●

52. IMPORTANCE OF TIME

LIFE is short and yet man spends it like a prodigal, as if it were eternal and he, immortal. Most of us do not understand the value of time, the most valuable gift from God. The waste of time we indulge in, is really surprising. Most of us have not been taught or told how to value and use this treasure called time. The precious minutes which can be turned to excellent use are wasted away in thoughtless and purposeless activities. If man takes care of his minutes then the hours and days will take care of themselves. Time is more precious than money. Time is universal and eternal. We all grow in time, live in time and ultimately perish in time. Time may not be defined exactly, but we all know what it is and how valuable.

Our life is a bubble, a short morning dream, brittle as glass and, therefore, we should take good care of it and make the best use. We all want fame, success, happiness, and prosperity but only a few are able to achieve this because only they make the best use of their time. Time and tide wait for none. They cannot be commanded. They are to be used in the best possible manner. We should be prepared to make the best use of an opportunity when offered. Time once lost can never be recovered. The flow of time is ceaseless and eternal and we all are like small, insignificant and helpless particles in this endless and continuous flow. Time is destiny. It is more powerful than the most powerful monarchs, princes, and rulers. These come and go but time is forever, eternal, without an end, without any beginning. Time is creation, birth, growth, ageing, decay and also death. Nothing escapes time. Time is abstract but its footprints are concrete and palpable. Time may be spent wisely or foolishly. The choice is ours and so are its consequences. It is the basic building block that goes in making our success, career, happiness, and status in society.

Shakespeare has declared in a clarion call :

There is a tide in the affairs of man
Which, taken at the flood, leads on to fortune;
Omitted, all the voyage of their life
Is bound in shallows and miseries.
On such a full sea we are afloat,
And we must take the current when its serves,
Or lose our ventures.

All great and successful men and women have been great economisers of time. They never squandered their evenings, mornings, afternoons or nights but used them in the best possible way. This helped them to not only find place in the history of mankind but could also change its course. They have left their footprints on the sands of time :

Lives of all great men remind us
We can make our lives sublime
And, departing, leave behind us
Footprints on the sands of time.

We should try to follow these great and successful people, the heroes of history, the guiding stars of humanity.

It is foolishness to think that we can make up for lost time. The past is dead and the future unborn. There are no tomorrows and yesterdays. It is today which is important. It is really sad that people spend their present in repenting over the uselessly spent past. Shelley has underlined this tragic fact so beautifully, thus :

We look before and after,
And pine for what is not :
Our sweetest laughter,
With some pain is fraught :
Our sweetest songs are those
That tell of saddest thoughts.

It makes one sad and hopeless to think how all the teachings, sayings and fables of the wise, the sages, the seers, the poets, the divinities, and great men of learning and letters have been of no avail in the matter. We waste our precious moments either grieving over the past blunders or making castles in the air for the future. In other words, we waste today in fretting over the dead yesterday, or in day-dreaming about tomorrow, which yet does not exist at all. And it reminds the well-known and oft quoted lines of Macbeth, the famous tragedy of Shakespeare :

Tomorrow, and tomorrow, and the tomorrow, creeps in this petty peace from day-to-day
To the last syllable of recorded time,
And all our yesterdays have lighted fools
The way to dusty death.

Men are great, good and famous in proportion of the time best utilised. All men and women of substance make the best use of time and opportunity. In this context, it has been beautifully said that, 'Time wasted is mere existence, used is life'. How many of us are really alive in this sense is the million dollar question? Time is eternal, boundless, endless and without either end or beginning but for us, as individuals, it is very limited, finite and short-lived. You can neither borrow nor steal nor earn time. When we say 'A stitch in time saves nine', we say the same thing idiomatically. A work done in time is time earned; a decisive action at a given moment is vital.

Successful men and women seldom talk of leisure because they hardly have any time to spare. Their every moment is well planned. It is the idler who has sufficient time to gossip, to indulge in loose talk, to rue the lost past and to build castles in the air for the future. Such people should heed the advice of the poet :

Think not a trifle, though it small appear,
Small sands make the mountain, moments make the year,
And trifles, life.

A proper use of time means the right use of an opportunity. Remember, time is money. It is precious and it waits for none. How important are small moments in life is again underlined in the following lines of poetry :

Little drops of water,
Little grains of sand,
Make the mighty ocean
And the beauteous land
And the little moments

Humble though they be,
Make the mighty ages
of eternity.

Opportunities are few and far between. That is why they are rare and called golden. The wise make the best use of them when they occur. Those of us who miss them or fail to recognise them in time, have to repent all our life. It also implies that we should be punctual and regular in our work-schedule. Nothing should be done in fits and starts. We are often plagued with lethargy, passivity, indecision, procrastination and vacillation and these are our greatest enemies. ●